Part 1
through P-51C

P-51
Mustang

A DETAIL & SCALE
AVIATION PUBLICATION

in detail & scale

Bert Kinzey

squadron/signal publications

COPYRIGHT © 1996 BY DETAIL & SCALE, INC.

This book is a product of Detail & Scale, Inc., which has sole responsibility for its content and layout, except that all contributors are responsible for the security clearance and copyright release of all materials submitted. Published by Squadron/Signal Publications, 1115 Crowley Drive, Carrollton, Texas 75011.

CONTRIBUTORS AND SOURCES:

Jeff Ethell

Dave Menard

Lloyd Jones

Jim Roeder

John Paul

Bill Bosworth

Merle Olmstead

Jerry Gabe

Walt Fink

Stan Parker

Lonnie Berry

Warren Munkasy

The United States Air Force Museum

The Yanks Air Museum

North American Aviation

The United States Air Force

The author and Detail & Scale express a sincere appreciation to Stanton Hoefler of the Yanks Air Museum at Chino, California. Stan's cooperation and patience were instrumental in obtaining access to the museum's beautifully restored P-51A. David Gallup, also of Yanks, deserves thanks for his efforts as well. Detail & Scale highly recommends this excellent museum to all aviation enthusiasts.

Many photographs in this publication are credited to their contributors. Photographs with no credit indicated were taken by the author.

Above: (Front cover photograph) The classic and aerodynamic lines of the Mustang are revealed in this dramatic photo of a P-51B-1-NA flying over water. **(NAA)**

Right: (Rear cover photograph) Cockpit colors and details in a P-51A are revealed in this close-up view of the instrument panel.

INTRODUCTION

This front view of one of the XP-51s shows the aircraft shortly after it was completed. Note the fairings for the wing and chin guns, although no armament was installed at the time this photo was taken. Both XP-51s were taken from the Mustang I production, so details, including the armament layout, were very similar between the Mustang Is and the two XP-51s. *(USAFM)*

As volume 50, this title marks a milestone in the Detail & Scale Series. It exemplifies the success and longevity of a series of aviation publications designed primarily to illustrate and explain the physical details of aircraft. Previously, only two series of aviation books have reached their fiftieth volume. But volume 50 is also a first in that it is the initial title in the series to be produced and distributed with Squadron/Signal Publications as the publisher. This is just as significant as reaching the fiftieth volume, because it represents a rebirth of the series and will make these books available to more aviation enthusiasts than ever before.

Of all the subjects covered in previous books in this series, none has had more information published about it than the P-51 Mustang. Indeed, so much has been written about North American's famous fighter, that it would not be unjustified for a person to wonder why anyone would want to write another book about it. However, what has not been published about the Mustang is a close-up, detailed look at the aircraft or clear, concise explanations about the differences between the variants. Even among people who study aircraft, very few know which versions of the Allison-powered Mustangs had chin-mounted machine guns, or which had cannon armament. It is this look at all Mustang variants that Detail & Scale has set out to produce.

As information was gathered for this publication, it became quickly apparent that all Mustang versions could not be contained in one volume. It is therefore necessary to divide the coverage between two books. Versions up through the P-51C are included in this first part, and volume 51 will cover the P-51D and subsequent variants as part two.

Considerable effort has been made to provide complete coverage of every important detail of the Mustang's design and to illustrate the differences between

variants. Several restored aircraft were visited, and features which accurately reflect the original specifications were photographed extensively. Dozens of photographs, taken specifically for this publication, are included. Existing vintage photographs also have captions that point out details and differences. The most extensive detailed coverage is provided for the P-51A beginning on page 41. Other variants have detailed photographs that illustrate their differences from the P-51A. Where details remain the same, they are usually not shown again.

The text is also written primarily to explain and point out the design's features and changes from variant to variant. Also important are the ten pages of 1/72nd scale drawings that were done by aviation illustrator Lloyd Jones specifically for this publication. Complete four-view plans are provided for the Mustang I, P-51, and P-51A. Five-view scale drawings are included for the A-36 and the P-51B/C. Supplemental views are also provided for the P-51B/C. We believe these to be the most complete and accurate scale drawings ever made available to the public.

Finally, a summary table can be found on page 10 which concisely compares all major differences between the variants from the NA-73X through the P-51B/C. Never before has this information been brought together in one place so it can be studied and compared easily.

For the scale modeler, the modelers section at the end of the book reviews all available kits of the Mustang variants covered in this publication. These include kits dating back over thirty years to ones released just as this book was published.

Other books cover the Mustang's use in combat, the pilots who flew it, and the markings it carried. But for aviation enthusiasts who want to study the physical details of all Mustang variants, this volume, and the one that follows, provide the most in-depth look at these features ever published.

HISTORICAL DEVELOPMENT

The NA-73X prototype was ready to fly only six months after design work began. Most of the major features seen on this aircraft were retained throughout the entire Mustang production run, and this is clear evidence of the excellent planning and sound judgement that went into the design. *(NAA via Jones)*

In the early months of 1940, America's entry into World War II was still nearly two years away. But on the European continent, nothing seemed to be able to slow the onslaught of the German military as one country after another came under Nazi control. It appeared to be only a matter of time, and perhaps a very short time, before England would be facing the German war machine alone.

Great Britain needed the weapons and materials of war in great quantity, and it needed them quickly. Nothing was of higher priority than fighter planes to defend the island nation, and in January 1940, before the fall of France, the Anglo French Purchasing Commission came to America hoping to acquire additional P-40s. But the Curtiss production lines were operating at capacity, so some "back room" discussions sent them to see James H. "Dutch" Kindelberger, the president of North American Aviation.

The British had purchased aircraft from North American before, but they had been trainers, not the fighters they now so desperately needed. In fact, up to that time, North American had never produced a true fighter design. During World War II, it would later become common for one company to produce another's design. Vega and Douglas would build Boeing's B-17, Goodyear would build Vought's Corsair, General Motors would build Grumman's Wildcat and Avenger, and Curtiss would even build Republic's Thunderbolts. But in 1940, North American was not interested in producing Curtiss P-40s for the British.

Instead, North American informed the British that

it could produce an even better fighter plane than the P-40, while still using the same Allison V-1710 inline engine. Reports have been published stating that North American stipulated in the contract that this would be accomplished in only 120 days, but in fact, there was no such guarantee in the contract. Nevertheless, North American did assure the British that the plane could be designed and produced very quickly.

On 10 April, 1940, the proposal was accepted, and the prototype, assigned North American's model number NA-73, was ordered. The following month, France fell to the Germans, and England was indeed alone. Soon, a small number of Spitfires and Hurricanes would begin the defense of England against the Luftwaffe in the Battle of Britain. Britain's need for fighters was never more desperate.

Asked to name the American military personnel who made significant contributions to victory in World War II, men like Dwight Eisenhower, George Patton, Douglas MacArthur, and Chester Nimitz would be on most lists. But a very good argument could also be made to include First Lieutenant Benjamin S. Kelsey. Lt. Kelsey was head of the Army Air Corps Pursuit Projects Office at Wright Field, and he was the single most important man in the acquisition of what would eventually become the P-51 Mustang fighter. With a degree in aeronautical engineering from M.I.T., Kelsey was qualified in aircraft design and performance, and he ingeniously found the means and the money to keep the program going until America's entry into the war insured its success.

On 4 May, 1940, when North American obtained release to sell the NA-73 to the British, Kelsey had included the stipulation that two aircraft from the first production batch would be turned over to Wright Field for testing. This meant that the British would buy the U. S. Army two aircraft which it did not then have the funds to purchase for itself.

Kelsey also knew of the National Advisory Committee on Aeronautics' (the forerunner to NASA) studies on the laminar flow airfoil, and as an aeronautical engineer, he understood its importance to new aircraft design and performance. As a result, NACA's Eastman Jacobs was assigned to North American's team that was working on the new fighter for the British. Raymond H. Rice was North American's Chief Engineer, Edgar Schmued their Chief of Design, and Ed Horkey was the aerodynamicist. Along with Jacobs, they worked day and night, seven days a week, to produce the new fighter as quickly as possible.

Curtiss had been ordered to turn over its design studies and other pertinent information on the XP-46. This included the radiator scoop originally intended for installation under the fuselage of the P-40. This scoop, which provided cooling air for glycol and oil cooling, was also to have a hot air exit ramp which would create thrust that more than offset the drag caused by the frontal cross section for the scoop. Though never fitted operationally to the P-40, it held promise and was one of the features incorporated in the design of the NA-73.

Just how much the data from Curtiss was used is subject to debate. Curtiss engineers state that it was almost total, while those at North American claim that little of the information was used. The truth is probably somewhere between these two extremes. Clearly, the NA-73 had a lot in common with the XP-46, and a rational analysis would indicate that the NA-73 could not have been engineered in such a short period of time without considerable use of the Curtiss data. But equally as clear is the original thinking added by the North American design team. Among the most important changes was the addition of the laminar flow wing.

On 9 September, 1940, only 102 days after the contract had been signed, the NA-73X prototype was rolled out though still waiting for its engine. The new

fighter was named Mustang by the British and the first British version was designated Mustang I. As soon as it was available, the 1,120-horsepower Allison V-1710-39 powerplant was installed, and engine and taxi tests began. On 26 October, Vance Breese lifted the aircraft off the runway for a maiden flight. Testing continued until Paul Balfour was forced to make a dead stick landing. The NA-73X flipped over on its back, and it took six weeks to make repairs and get the aircraft ready to fly again. The first production Mustang I soon joined the repaired prototype in the test program, and shortly other Mustangs were heading for England.

As expected, the evaluation of the flight test aircraft showed that the NA-73 was indeed superior to the P-40 Warhawk which was considered to be the best single-engine fighter in the U. S. Army Air Corps inventory at the time. A lot of criticism has been written about the AAC's initial lack of interest and subsequent slowness to act concerning acquiring Mustangs for its own use. This simply is not so. All evidence is to the contrary, particularly considering the political and economic situation in America at that time. Here again Lt. Benjamin Kelsey was the man who deserves the credit.

As stated earlier, Kelsey saw to it that two aircraft from the original British order were supplied to Wright Field for testing, but his efforts did not stop there. Kelsey was able to place an order for 150 P-51s on 7 July, 1941, and this was before the first XP-51 even arrived in Ohio. It was a small order for the first U. S. version, but it was all that funding would allow at that time.

The P-51 was very similar to the Mustang I, with the main difference being the replacement of the mixed machine gun armament of the British version with four 20-mm cannon. Clearly, the USAAC had a genuine interest in the NA-73, even before it had a chance to obtain one. The situation in Europe would cause ninety-three of the P-51s to be sent to the Royal Air Force where they were called Mustang IAs.

With an order from the U. S. Army, North American chose the nickname "Apache" for the U. S. aircraft. But by then the British name, Mustang, had taken root, and it became the official nickname of the USAAC.

With no funds available for pursuit aircraft, as

The first production variant was the Mustang I which was used exclusively by the British. It was armed with a total of eight machine guns, including four .50-caliber and four .30-caliber weapons. Two of the .50-caliber guns were chin-mounted in the nose, while the other six guns were located in the wings. This is AG348, the second Mustang I built, and it was one of two Mustang Is turned over to the USAAF for evaluation as XP-51s. Note the original short carburetor intake scoop on the top of the nose. (USAFM)

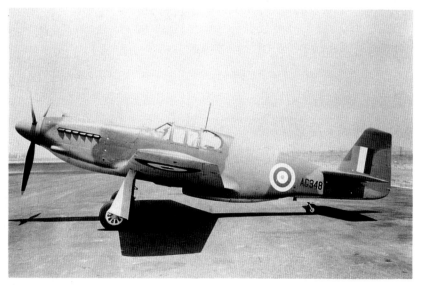

This is the same aircraft seen in the bottom photograph on the previous page. It has been modified to XP-51 standards for evaluation by the USAAF. Note the longer carburetor intake scoop on the nose. (USAFM)

A rear view of one of the XP-51 prototypes reveals more of its markings and details. Note how much more wear the anti-skid walkway on the left wing has received as compared to the walkway on the right wing. (USAFM)

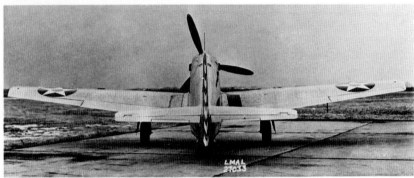

The first Mustang variant to be produced for the USAAF was designated simply the P-51. Called the Mustang IA by the British, this version deleted the machine gun armament of the Mustang I, and replaced it with four 20-mm cannon. (USAFM)

Six .50-caliber machine guns, two of which were chin-mounted in the nose, armed the A-36 ground attack version of the Mustang. Unofficially called the Apache and the Invader, this variant was also fitted with dive brakes to allow it to perform the dive bomber role. One was delivered to England for testing, but this type was never ordered for British service.
(NAA via Jones)

The P-51A deleted the two chin guns and the dive brakes of the A-36. It retained the four .50-caliber machine guns in the wings as its only internal armament. However, the P-51A also kept the under-wing pylons of the A-36. External fuel tanks, or bombs up to the 500-pound class, could be loaded on these external hardpoints. This variant was called Mustang II by the British. (USAFM)

fighters were then called, Lt. Kelsey came up with a way to beat the system and get some additional Mustangs on order for the USAAC. Using some remaining funds for attack aircraft, Kelsey asked North American to develop a dive bomber version of the NA-73. Choosing A-36, which was the next available attack designation, Kelsey ordered 500 of these dive bomber versions on 16 April, 1942. Ironically, the North American name, "Apache," was commonly used with the A-36 but never officially recognized by the newly renamed U. S. Army Air Forces.

About a month and a half after the order for 150 P-51s had been made on 7 July, 1941, the first XP-51 arrived at Wright Field on 24 August. The second did not join the first until 16 December. In between these deliveries, the Japanese had caused everything in the United States to change with their attack at Pearl Harbor. No one could claim any longer that this was Mr. Hitler and Mr. Churchill's war. It was World War II.

As America moved swiftly from a peacetime to wartime footing, there were a lot of important things to do amidst all the chaos. Priorities had to be established, and where fighters were concerned, top priority had to be given to producing large numbers of the fighters then on the production lines. This meant that numbers were more important than testing, and it was essential to get the aircraft industry turning out every available fighter as quickly as possible. Doing so would get more P-38s, P-39s, and P-40s into combat at the earliest possible date. Pilots had to be trained to fly these planes, and ground crews had to be taught how to maintain them. Meanwhile, the Navy wanted more ships, the Army wanted more tanks and artillery pieces, and all needed more trained bodies. Some things just had to wait until more people became available to handle everything that needed to be done.

The British had fitted some of their Mustang Is with cameras for use in the tactical reconnaissance role. The USAAF began doing the same thing as soon as P-51s became available. Known as F-6As, these camera laden aircraft were the first U. S Mustangs to see combat with the 154th Observation Squadron in North Africa.

The last Allison-powered Mustang was the P-51A. It was fitted with the Allison V-1710-81 engine and was very much like the A-36 without the dive-bombing equipment or the chin-mounted machine guns. However it did retain the under-wing racks for bombs and external fuel tanks. A total of 310 were built, and of these fifty

were sent to the RAF as Mustang IIs. Thirty-five others were fitted with cameras and designated F-6Bs.

In numerous accounts about the development of the Allison-powered Mustang, it has been stated that its poor performance at high altitudes was a surprise and a disappointment to the British and to the USAAF as well. This simply is not so. The aircraft designers of that day had more than sufficient knowledge of powerplants, and they were capable of determining that the Allison engine and supercharger combination installed in the aircraft would have a drop in performance above 15,000 feet. Clear evidence of this is that two of the P-51s, ordered even before the flight of the first XP-51, were reserved for testing with a Packard-built Rolls Royce Merlin engine. They knew that the Allison-powered Mustangs would be low-level fighters, while the Merlin-powered aircraft would be the high-altitude versions. By comparison, Mustangs with the Allison engine could outperform the Merlin-powered variants below 15,000 feet, but no writer has criticized the P-51B, -C, -D, or -K for having less performance at low altitudes. It has been claimed that the Merlin engine is what allowed the Mustang to reach its potential. If only high-altitude performance is considered, this would be true. But a more correct assessment would be that both the Allison and Merlin-powered versions performed very well at the altitudes where they were designed and intended to operate.

The first production version of the Mustang to be equipped with the Merlin engine was the P-51B. Identical airframes were produced at North American's Dallas plant, and were designated P-51Cs. By the time these variants were ordered, America was in a full wartime economy, and production numbers of these Mustangs were in the thousands instead of the hundreds. The British received these two variants as well, and named them Mustang IIIs. Seventy-one P-51Bs and twenty P-51Cs were fitted with cameras and designated F-6Cs.

During the second half of 1942 and much of 1943, U. S. heavy bombers suffered great losses as they flew unescorted, daylight missions over enemy territory. The new, high-altitude versions of the Mustang have been heralded as the savior of the bombing campaign. But it must be understood that the reason the bombers were not escorted by fighters during the early months of America's involvement in the European Theater was a matter of choice and not because of a lack of adequate fighters.

When he was in command of the 8th Air Force,

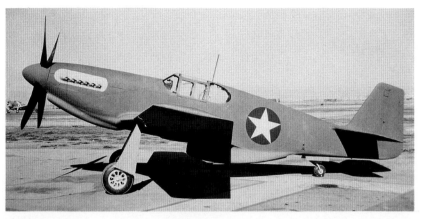

The first of two XP-51Bs is shown here with the Merlin engine installed. Noticeable differences over the Allison-powered Mustangs include the larger radiator scoop under the fuselage, the carburetor intake scoop being moved from the top to the bottom of the nose, and the four-bladed Hamilton Standard propeller. Both XP-51Bs were converted from P-51 airframes. (NAA via Jones)

General Ira Eaker did not believe the bombers needed escort. He thought that the bombers' defensive armament would be protection enough. High rates of losses never deterred him from this belief. Accordingly, Eaker turned down the P-38 Lightnings provided him to protect his bombers. The P-38s, with enough range to escort the bombers to any of their targets, spent time in England with relatively little to do, and many were subsequently sent to Africa.

It might be argued that the Lightning did not have adequate performance to match the enemy fighters. Evidence also proves this to be untrue. Although powered with the Allison V-1710 engine, the Lightning was provided with excellent superchargers, so it was a very capable fighter at high altitudes. Its range equaled or bettered that of the Mustang and was continually increased with each new version. An experienced pilot could fly the Lightning successfully against any fighter that the Germans or Japanese had. The top two American Aces of the war, Richard Bong with forty victories, and Thomas McGuire with thirty-eight, both scored all of their kills in the P-38 against some of the better Japanese pilots who were flying very maneuverable and capable fighters. German and Japanese documents captured after the war also indicated that both considered the P-38 a formidable adversary. So from the beginning, the Lightning was available with the range necessary to escort the bombers. It had the performance to mix it up with the enemy, but Eaker didn't want it. The bombers were not escorted until General "Hap" Arnold replaced Eaker with Jimmy Doolittle.

This is not to take anything away from the Mustang or its contributions. It was an excellent fighter that made a significant contribution to the war wherever it

Careful examination of this factory-fresh P-51B will reveal a white + beneath the data plate on the side of the fuselage. This +, which was sometimes white and other times black, indicated that the aircraft was fitted with a fuselage fuel tank. This tank shifted the aircraft's center of gravity to a dangerous point, and the + helped remind the pilot to be weary of this condition. (USAFM)

served. What has been explained here is only to put the facts in proper perspective and dispute the myth that there was no fighter capable of escorting the bombers prior to the P-51B. It was a matter of choice, not availability.

The Mustang did have three points in its favor. First, a pilot could learn to fly it to a high level of proficiency faster than the pilot of the twin-engined P-38. Second, it was simple and therefore easier to maintain. Third, and perhaps most important, its simple design could

In spite of damage to its vertical tail and rudder, this P-51B returned to its base safely. Note the invasion stripes around the wings and fuselage. Later these would be painted out on the upper surfaces. The 6N fuselage code indicates that this Mustang is assigned to the 504th Fighter Squadron of the 339th Fighter Group. (USAFM)

One of the complaints about early Mustangs concerned the original flush canopy. It did not provide excellent all-around visibility, nor did it afford very good access to the cockpit. The left side window hinged downward, and the top hinged up on the right side. This meant that no access to the cockpit could be made from the right wing without removing part of the canopy. *(USAFM)*

An important modification to some Mustangs fitted with the flush canopy was the installation of what became known as the Malcolm hood. This semi-bubble canopy provided much improved visibility, and because it slid aft, it allowed for easier access to the cockpit from both sides. *(USAFM)*

be mass produced in great numbers relatively quickly. Large numbers of fighters were going to be required as the huge bomber raids were staged during the last year of the war in Europe.

A very unpopular feature on all Mustangs up through the P-51C was the standard flush canopy. This canopy only opened to the left, and its framework restricted the pilot's view. An interim solution to this problem was the use of the British-developed Malcolm hood. This semi-bubble canopy slid aft on rails, thus affording easy access to the cockpit from both sides. It

also offered unrestricted visibility to both sides and above the aircraft. But the Malcolm canopy was available in limited quantities and not fitted on many aircraft.

The ultimate solution to the visibility problem was first tested on P-51B, 43-12102. It was modified with a cut down rear fuselage and a teardrop-shaped, full bubble canopy. This canopy provided excellent all-around visibility for the Mustang pilot, and it became a standard feature on the P-51D and all subsequent variants. It is these Mustangs that will be covered in The P-51 Mustang in Detail & Scale, Part 2.

The ultimate solution to the visibility problems connected with the original flush canopy began with P-51B-1-NA, 43-12102. This aircraft was modified with a cut down rear fuselage and a true bubble canopy for test purposes. These changes resulted in the production of the P-51D and subsequent versions of the Mustang, all of which had bubble canopies. Note that all other features of this aircraft remain as -B standards to include the wing. The design of the wing for the P-51D was changed from what is seen here.

(NAA via Jones)

MUSTANG VARIANTS
MAIN DIFFERENCES TABLE
(NA-73X THROUGH P-51B/C AIRCRAFT)

NAA MODEL	NA-73X	NA-73 & NA-83	NA-91	NA-97	NA-99	NA-102, 103, 104
U.S. DESIGNATION	NONE	XP-51	P-51	A-36A	P-51A	P-51B & P-51C
BRITISH DESIGNATION	NONE	MUSTANG I	MUSTANG IA	NONE	MUSTANG II	MUSTANG III
ARMAMENT	NONE	2 X .50 CAL. MG IN CHIN + 2 X .50 CAL. & 4 X .30 CAL. MG IN WINGS	4 X 20mm CANNON IN WINGS	2 X .50 CAL. MG IN CHIN + 4 X .50 CAL. MG IN WINGS	4 X .50 CAL. MG IN WINGS	4 X .50 CAL. MG IN WINGS
ENGINE	ALLISON V-1710-39	ALLISON V-1710-39	ALLISON V-1710-V-39	ALLISON V-1710-87	ALLISON V-1710-81	PACKARD MERLIN V-1650-3/-7
CARBURETOR SCOOP	THIN & SHORT ON TOP OF NOSE	THIN & LONG ON TOP OF NOSE	THIN & LONG ON TOP OF NOSE	THICK & LONG ON TOP OF NOSE	THICK & LONG ON TOP OF NOSE	UNDER NOSE
COOLING AIR SCOOP	SHALLOW & HINGED	SHALLOW & HINGED	SHALLOW & HINGED	SHALLOW & FIXED	SHALLOW & FIXED	DEEP & FIXED
LANDING/TAXI LIGHTS	SINGLE LIGHT ON EACH WING	SINGLE LIGHT ON EACH WING	SINGLE LIGHT ON EACH WING	TWO LIGHTS IN ONE UNIT ON LEFT WING	SINGLE LIGHT ON LEFT WING	SINGLE LIGHT ON LEFT WING
PROPELLER	CURTISS ELECTRIC 3-BLADE 10' 6" DIAMETER	CURTISS ELECTRIC 3-BLADE 10' 6" (EARLY) 10' 9" (LATE)	CURTISS ELECTRIC 3-BLADE 10' 9" DIAMETER	CURTISS ELECTRIC 3-BLADE 10' 9" DIAMETER	CURTISS ELECTRIC 3-BLADE 10' 9" DIAMETER	HAMILTON STANDARD 4-BLADE 11' 2" DIAMETER
PITOT	L-SHAPED UNDER RIGHT WING	L-SHAPED UNDER RIGHT WING	L-SHAPED UNDER RIGHT WING	BOOM STYLE ON RIGHT WING	L-SHAPED UNDER RIGHT WING	L-SHAPED UNDER RIGHT WING
NUMBER BUILT	1	620	150	500	310	1988 P-51B 1750 P-51C
COMMENTS	CIVIL REGISTRY NX19998	2 XP-51s TAKEN FROM BRITISH MUSTANG I ORDER	93 TO BRITISH AS MUSTANG IA, 55 TO USAAF, 2 FOR MERLIN ENGINE TESTS AS XP-51B, PHOTO VERSION DESIGNATED F-6A	DIVE BRAKES ON TOPS AND BOTTOMS OF BOTH WINGS, TWO UNDERWING PYLONS	50 TO BRITISH AS MUSTANG II, REMAINDER TO USAAF, TWO UNDERWING PYLONS, PHOTO VERSION DESIGNATED F-6B	FUSELAGE FUEL TANK ADDED AT P-51B-10-NA & P-51C-5-NT, RETROFITTED TO SOME EARLIER PRODUCTION AIRCRAFT

There were a number of specific physical differences between the various Mustang versions covered in this book. An understanding of these differences is important, particularly to the scale modeler. While there are considerable reference sources available on these differences, they do not offer a concise side-by-side comparison. This table is provided here so that the major differences between these Mustang variants may be studied and compared on a single page. Photographs and descriptions of these various features may be found on the pages that cover each variant in more detail.

Natural metal P-51B Mustangs roll out of the North American plant during late 1943. In the foreground is a B-25 Mitchell medium bomber, which was another major contribution to the war effort made by North American.
(USAFM)

NA-73X

North American's Model NA-73X was the first Mustang built. Although armament was not fitted when this photograph was taken, the holes for the eight machine guns are visible. The fairing for one of the chin-mounted machine guns can be seen just below the spinner, while the other is covered by a propeller blade. At first glance, there may appear to be only two holes in each leading edge for the machine guns, but the middle gun in each wing was located further aft and lower than the other two. The hole for the middle gun can be seen under each wing, and it is located between the two holes which are visible on each leading edge. Also note the L-shaped pitot probe under the right wing. This would remain standard on future Mustang versions except for the A-36. (NAA via Jones)

As soon as the British signed the contract with North American on 10 April, 1940, work began immediately on the single prototype that would be the sire of the entire line of Mustangs. Designated Model NA-73X at North American, this airframe would be rolled out, still waiting for its engine, only 102 days later. The major lines in that aircraft's design would remain constant with very little in the way of changes on all subsequent single-engine variants in the Mustang series.

Unique to the NA-73X was a one-piece, blown windscreen which had no internal framework. This would be replaced by a framed, bulletproof design on production aircraft. Although unarmed, fairings for the chin-mounted .50-caliber machine guns and holes for the wing guns were noticeable on the completed aircraft. It was given the civil registry of NX19998.

Once the Allison V-1710-39 engine arrived, it was installed in the aircraft, and taxi tests began. Then, on 26 October, 1940, Vance Breese lifted off the runway for a maiden flight lasting a brief five minutes. Flight testing began immediately, and the results were very promising. North American had made good on its promise to build a fighter that would outperform the Curtiss P-40 while using the same powerplant.

But on 20 November, the Allison engine quit during the ninth test flight, and Paul Balfour attempted a wheels-down landing in a soft field. The NA-73X flipped over on its back and came to rest upside down in the field. Balfour was unhurt, but the aircraft needed six weeks to repair. It was subsequently determined that the engine had quit due to fuel starvation. There had been nothing wrong with the aircraft itself. Once repaired, the NA-73X was joined by the first production Mustang I in the flight test program.

The natural metal NA-73X was devoid of any markings except that the civil registration number NX19998 was later lettered on the wings. Note the original short carburetor air scoop on the top of the nose. (NAA via Jones)

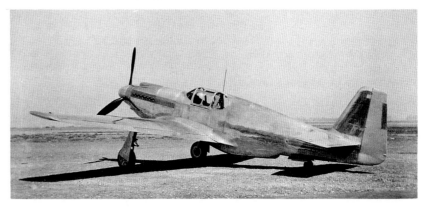

MUSTANG I

The defining characteristics of the Mustang I can be seen in this view. Note the hinged radiator intake scoop in the lowered position beneath the fuselage. This feature remained on the P-51, but was deleted on the P-51A and A-36. There is a single landing/taxi light on the leading edge of each wing, and this is another feature that the Mustang I shared only with the P-51. Also noteworthy is the eight-gun armament of mixed caliber. The two chin-mounted .50-caliber weapons have fairings where they enter the nose. The A-36 also had the chin-mounted guns, but the fairings were not present. The other six guns, consisting of two more .50-caliber and four .30-caliber, were located in the wings. Note again how the center of the three guns in each wing is mounted lower than the other two. This aircraft is British serial number AG347, which was the third Mustang I in the first production batch. It was originally built with the short carburetor scoop on top of the nose but was retrofitted with the longer production scoop by the time this photograph was taken.
(Ethell collection)

On 29 May, 1940, the British placed an order for 320 aircraft which it designated the Mustang I. These aircraft were assigned the British serial numbers AG345 through AG664. A second order for an additional 300 Mustang Is had serial numbers AL958 through AL999, AM100 through AM257, and AP164 through AP263.

For the most part, this first production variant differed little from the NA-73X. A framed, bulletproof windscreen replaced the blown design used on the prototype, and the carburetor intake scoop on top of the nose was lengthened to a point just aft of the spinner beginning with the fourth production Mustang I. This change was retrofitted to the first three aircraft as well. Testing also indicated the need to enlarge the cooling air scoop beneath the fuselage. Like the NA-73X, the Mustang I retained the hinged scoop which could be opened for increased cooling during engine run-ups and taxiing. The addition of self-sealing fuel tanks was the only other major

difference between the prototype and these first production airframes. Like the NA-73X, the Mustang I had a single landing/taxi light installed in the leading edge of each wing, just outboard of the guns.

The British wanted a heavily armed fighter with a mixed battery of eight machine guns. Two .50-caliber guns were mounted beneath the engine in the nose section, while the other two .50-caliber guns and four .30-caliber weapons were located in the wings.

The first flight of a Mustang I took place on 23 April, 1941, and the first example joined the repaired NA-73X in the test and evaluation program. Contractual arrangements with the British called for two of the Mustang Is to be turned over to the USAAC for test and evaluation.

The Mustang I began service with Number 2 Squadron in July 1942, and it immediately proved that it could outperform any other British fighter below 15,000

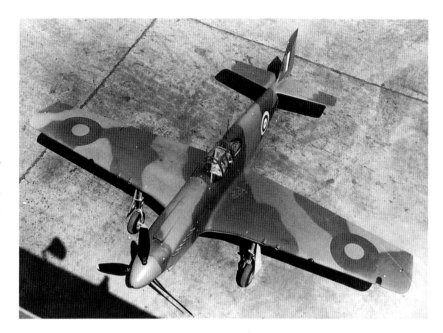

This overhead view illustrates the camouflage pattern on the first Mustang I. Again, note the single landing/taxi light on the leading edge of each wing as well as the small fairings for the inner and outer guns. The early short, thin, carburetor intake is evident on this aircraft. **(USAFM)**

feet. Indeed, its only limitation was its service ceiling, which was not unexpected given the powerplant and supercharger installed. But plans were already underway to develop high-altitude versions of the fighter with a different engine and supercharger combination.

The British fitted camera installations into some of their Mustang Is and found the aircraft ideally suited for the tactical reconnaissance role. One camera was usually mounted in the rear of the cockpit, while a second was installed in the rear fuselage aft of the radiator.

The British serial number AP247 in the fuselage band indicates that this Mustang I was part of the second production batch of Mustang Is supplied to England.
(Ethell collection)

MUSTANG I

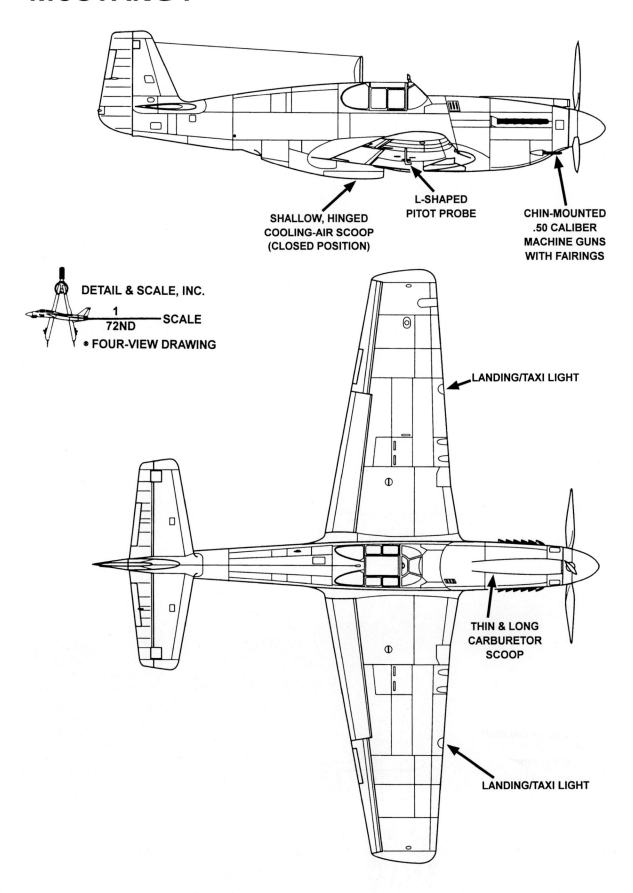

SHALLOW, HINGED
COOLING-AIR SCOOP
(CLOSED POSITION)

L-SHAPED
PITOT PROBE

CHIN-MOUNTED
.50 CALIBER
MACHINE GUNS
WITH FAIRINGS

DETAIL & SCALE, INC.

$\dfrac{1}{72ND}$ SCALE

• FOUR-VIEW DRAWING

LANDING/TAXI LIGHT

THIN & LONG
CARBURETOR
SCOOP

LANDING/TAXI LIGHT

DETAIL & SCALE, 1/72nd SCALE, COPYRIGHT DRAWING BY LLOYD JONES

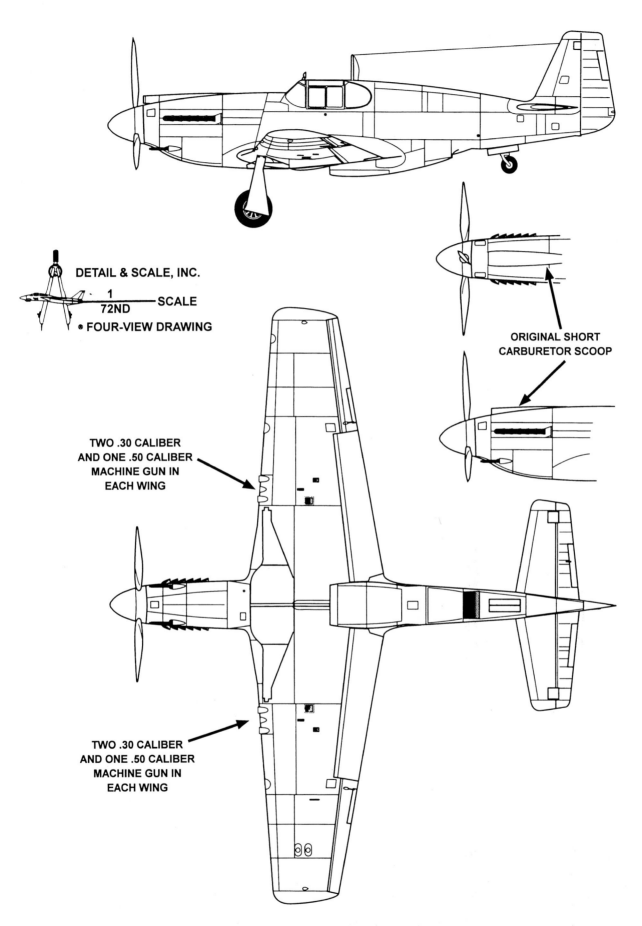

DETAIL & SCALE, INC.

$\dfrac{1}{72\text{ND}}$ SCALE

• FOUR-VIEW DRAWING

TWO .30 CALIBER
AND ONE .50 CALIBER
MACHINE GUN IN
EACH WING

ORIGINAL SHORT
CARBURETOR SCOOP

TWO .30 CALIBER
AND ONE .50 CALIBER
MACHINE GUN IN
EACH WING

DETAIL & SCALE, 1/72nd SCALE, COPYRIGHT DRAWING BY LLOYD JONES

The first of two XP-51 prototypes is shown here with USAAF markings on its wings and rudder. Armament provisions were the same as for the Mustang I, because both XP-51s came from the British Mustang I order. **(USAFM)**

When the Anglo-French Purchasing Commission came to the United States in early 1940, they were in desperate need of fighter aircraft. While not as severe as those faced by the British, the U. S. military also had its problems. There was a shortage of personnel, and there was the ever-present lack of funding in spite of the war clouds on the horizon. So when the British contracted with North American to build the Mustang I, it was stipulated that two of the aircraft would be turned over to the U. S. Army Air Corps for test and evaluation. Thus, the British paid for these two test aircraft for the United States.

Designated XP-51s and assigned the serial numbers 41-038 and 41-039, these two Mustangs were sent to Wright Field, Ohio, for test and evaluation. The first arrived on 24 August, 1941, while the second did not arrive until a few months later on 16 December. By then, things were in chaos within the U. S. military. There was

still a lack of funds and personnel, but the entire country was in the process of changing over from a peacetime to a wartime footing. Priorities had to be established, and the top consideration had to be given to those fighters already rolling off the lines. Accordingly, the evaluation of the new XP-51s could not and did not begin right away.

But as the two XP-51s began test flights, their capabilities, already demonstrated by the British Mustang Is, were again confirmed. Compared to the P-40, which was then considered the best single-engined fighter in the inventory, the XP-51 was superior in almost every performance criteria. The Americans were not happy with the mixed battery of guns chosen by the British, so one XP-51 was sent to Eglin Field, Florida, for gun tests. Ultimately, four 20-mm cannon were selected for what would become the first U. S. variant of the Mustang. XP-51, 41-038, also spent some time at Langley Field, Virginia, with the NACA for aerodynamic testing.

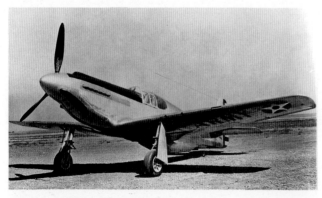

The same aircraft shown above is seen here at an earlier date. Note the original short carburetor scoop on the top of the nose. "U. S. ARMY" was painted under the wings along with the national insignia. **(USAFM)**

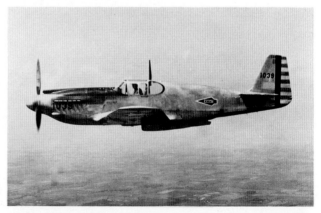

The famous Wright arrowhead was painted on both sides of the aft fuselage of the second XP-51 during flight testing at Wright field. **(USAFM)**

P-51 & MUSTANG IA

With its four large cannon clearly evident, a P-51 has its engine run up for checks prior to a flight. **(USAFM)**

On 7 July, 1941, the Army placed an order with North American for 150 P-51s. No suffix letter was placed after the P-51 designation. This order, while conservative in size, was made even though the two XP-51s had not yet arrived at Wright Field. This is clear evidence that the United States already recognized the significant potential of the design and was ready to commit to it as much as the available, but very limited, funds would permit.

Out of the 150 ordered, two were held back for

More features of the P-51 can be seen in this overhead view. Although not apparent here, the P-51 did retain the movable radiator intake scoop of the earlier Mustang I. It also had the single landing/taxi light on the leading edge of each wing, and these were located just outboard of the cannon.

(USAFM)

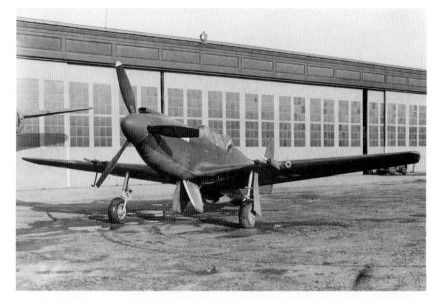

Most P-51s were fitted with cameras in the rear of the cockpit and redesignated F-6As. The bulged window for the camera can be seen in this photograph of a P-51 taken at Wright Field during testing. *(USAFM)*

eventual testing with the Merlin engine. Here again is evidence that the U. S. clearly recognized the value of the design, and was planning for the future where it was concerned. It was already known and understood that with the Allison engine and the turbocharger installed, these early Mustangs were excellent low-level fighters. However, they lacked excellent performance at higher altitudes. The fact that the Army retained these two P-51s for Merlin engine tests is unmistakable proof that it was already planning to develop high-altitude versions of the fighter as soon as possible. Further, the claims that the U. S. was not interested in the Mustang, and that its testing and evaluation were mishandled, cannot be substantiated by documented facts.

Ninety-three examples of this production run went to the British who dubbed them Mustang IAs. This designation was because the design did not differ from the Mustang I enough to justify an entirely new model number.

The remaining fifty-five P-51s were retained for service with the newly renamed U. S. Army Air Force. They also retained many of the features of the British Mustang I. These included the single landing/taxi light on the leading edge of each wing and the hinged cooling-air inlet scoop. But the mixed battery of machine guns had been replaced with four 20-mm cannon mounted in pairs in the wings. The chin-mounted machine guns of the Mustang I were deleted.

Like the British had done with their Mustangs, the USAAF installed cameras in its P-51s and redesignated them F-6As. The first combat use of any Mustang variant by the USAAF was during April 1943. The mission was flown in Africa by the 154th Observation Squadron using a camera-equipped F-6A.

Details of the camera installation can be seen here. The rear window on the left side was molded with a prominent bulge in order to accommodate the large camera. A flat circular piece of glass fitted over the lens. Other cameras were small enough to fit inside the standard window, but a circular or oval-shaped hole was cut from the glass to prevent distortion in the photographs. *(USAFM)*

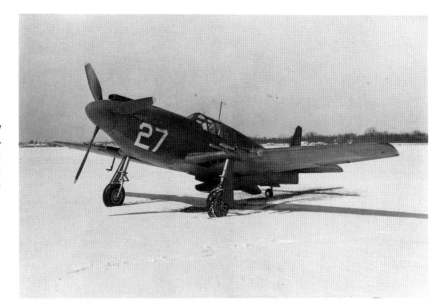

Neither the Mustang I or the P-51 had provisions for under-wing fuel tanks or ordnance. This left the aircraft in a particularly clean configuration for photography. (USAFM)

The hinged radiator scoop can be seen in the open position beneath the wing of this P-51. The scoop was opened to increase air flow to the radiator when the aircraft was being run up on the ground or as necessary during taxiing. It was kept in the up position during flight. (USAFM)

This close-up provides a better look at the hinged radiator scoop on a P-51. It is seen here in the lowered position. The P-51 shared this feature with the NA-73X, Mustang I, and the XP-51. The scoop was fixed on subsequent variants. (USAFM via Davis)

P-51 & MUSTANG IA

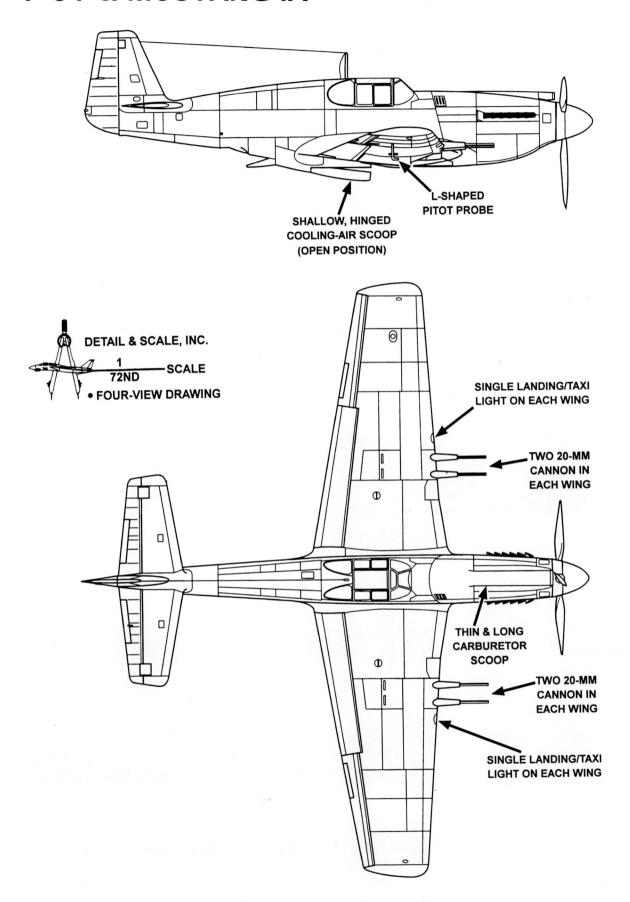

L-SHAPED
PITOT PROBE

SHALLOW, HINGED
COOLING-AIR SCOOP
(OPEN POSITION)

DETAIL & SCALE, INC.

1
──────── SCALE
72ND

● FOUR-VIEW DRAWING

SINGLE LANDING/TAXI
LIGHT ON EACH WING

TWO 20-MM
CANNON IN
EACH WING

THIN & LONG
CARBURETOR
SCOOP

TWO 20-MM
CANNON IN
EACH WING

SINGLE LANDING/TAXI
LIGHT ON EACH WING

DETAIL & SCALE, 1/72nd SCALE, COPYRIGHT DRAWING BY LLOYD JONES

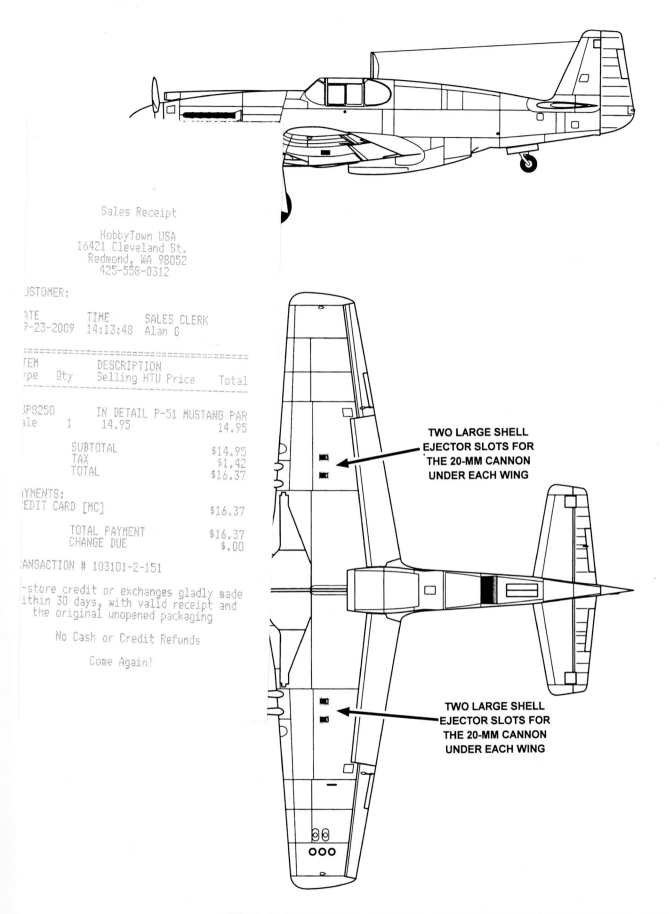

TWO LARGE SHELL
EJECTOR SLOTS FOR
THE 20-MM CANNON
UNDER EACH WING

TWO LARGE SHELL
EJECTOR SLOTS FOR
THE 20-MM CANNON
UNDER EACH WING

DETAIL & SCALE, 1/72nd SCALE, COPYRIGHT DRAWING BY LLOYD JONES

A-36

The A-36 was optimized for ground attack missions, and it was fitted with dive brakes so that it could serve as a dive bomber. Two bombs, up to 500-pounds in size, could be carried on pylons fitted under the wings. Although one example was given to Great Britain for evaluation, the British did not place an order for the A-36. The aircraft shown here was photographed in Africa and was assigned to the 27th Fighter-Bomber Group. A-36s were used extensively in Africa, Sicily, and Italy. (USAFM)

In mid-1941, just about everyone in the United States realized that war was eminent. But increased funding came very slowly. At the Pursuit Projects Office at Wright Field, Lt. Benjamin Kelsey had no money left for the development of pursuit aircraft, as fighters were then called. Tests of the NA-73X and the first Mustang I had confirmed the excellent low-level performance of the aircraft, so Kelsey came up with an idea to get the U. S. involved with the design. Choosing A-36, which was the next logical attack designation, Kelsey utilized some money allocated to ground attack aircraft. Although dive bombers were not popular with the Air Corps, and would never become so, the Germans had demonstrated the value of such aircraft with their Ju-87 Stuka. This seemed to be justification for money to be spent by the Army Air Corps to develop such an aircraft for itself. At least this was the excuse Kelsey used to keep the U. S. involved with the program.

To create a dive bomber version of the Mustang, dive brakes were added to the top and bottom of each wing. This necessitated relocating the L-shaped pitot probe, which was located under the right wing on the fighter versions. As a result, a pitot boom was installed on the wing's leading edge near the tip. Under-wing racks, which could carry 500-pound bombs, were mounted just outboard of the landing gear. These racks could also carry external fuel tanks as well. Like the Mustang I and P-51/Mustang IA, the A-36 had two landing/taxi lights. But these lights were not mounted as single units on each wing as had been the case with the earlier versions. Instead, both lights were located together in one large mounting on the leading edge of the left wing.

It was envisioned that the dive bomber would operate primarily at altitudes below 12,000 feet. To optimize performance at these altitudes, the Allison V-1710-87 engine was chosen. Although not dictated by the change in role from fighter to dive bomber, the radiator intake scoop was changed from the previous hinged design to a fixed inlet. An air filter was placed inside the carburetor scoop, and this resulted in a wider inlet than seen on previous versions.

To give the A-36 better firepower with which to strafe, the USAAC opted for six .50-caliber machine guns. Four of these were located in the wings in place of the P-

Two unique characteristics of the A-36 can be seen in these photographs. At left, the pitot boom on the leading edge of the right wing is visible. The A-36 was the only Mustang variant to use this type of pitot, while all others used the L-shaped pitot which was located under the right wing. At right, the dual-lens taxi/landing light can be seen in the leading edge of the left wing. This too was a feature unique to the A-36. The chin-mounted .50-caliber machine guns were a feature the A-36 shared only with the Mustang I, however, the A-36 did not have the fairings where the barrels of these weapons entered the fuselage. (Both USAFM)

No less that 150 mission markings are painted on the nose of this Apache from the 27th Fighter-Bomber Group. The photograph was taken at Gela, Sicily, in late 1943. (USAFM)

51's 20-mm cannon. The other two were chin-mounted as they had been on the Mustang I. However, the small fairings found on the earlier variant were not used on the A-36.

Lt. Kelsey's ingenuity and foresight kept the Army involved with the Mustang, and when funding became available for procurement, 500 A-36s were ordered by the USAAF on 16 April, 1942. This would be the largest order of Allison-powered Mustangs by the United States. Although one A-36 was shipped to England for evaluation, the British did not order this variant for the Royal Air Force.

North American initially chose the name "Apache" for the aircraft ordered by the United States. But the British name was already well established, and all U. S. machines also came to be known as Mustangs. But the A-36 was often referred to as the Apache, although it was unofficial as far as the USAAF was concerned. An attempt to call the A-36 the "Invader" by units in Sicily and

Italy also failed. That name was later applied to the Douglas A-26 instead. The official USAAF designation for the dive bomber was A-36A, but because there was no further development of the type, the "A" suffix was usually dropped.

The A-36 received its baptism of fire on 6 June, 1943, in North Africa. The 27th and 86th Fighter-Bomber Groups were the first to use it in action, and they later operated in Sicily and Italy. Although used primarily in the ground attack role as intended, A-36s flew escort missions as well.

In spite of the fact that it fought at low altitudes in the face of intense anti-aircraft fire from the ground, only 177 A-36s were lost in combat to enemy action. These losses came while flying more than 23,300 combat missions. That is an average of only one aircraft lost every 130 missions, and it is testimony not only to the design of the aircraft but to the ability of the pilots who flew it as well.

"Marge H," an A-36 from the 533rd Fighter Bomber Squadron of the 27th Fighter Bomber Group is shown during the war with her ground crew in the photograph at left. At right is a photograph of a restored A-36 at the Air Force Museum in Dayton, Ohio. Although the Air Force Museum chose to restore its A-36 using the markings applied to "Marge H" during the war, it is not the original aircraft as reported elsewhere. It is one of only two known A-36s still surviving.

(USAFM)

A-36 NOSE ART

"Dot" was an A-36 assigned to the 27th Fighter-Bomber Group. Note the open dive brakes on this aircraft as the pilot runs up the engine prior to taxiing out. A ground crewman sits on the wing to help guide the pilot as he taxis. (USAFM)

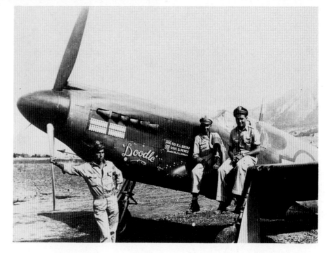

These two photographs are of the same A-36 which was piloted by Robert Bryant. The crew chief was SGT Dan Perry. The photo at left was taken in Sicily, while the one at right was taken in Pastuem, Italy, in November 1943.

(Both USAFM)

"Manaleene" was flown by Mark A. "Doc" Savage. This A-36 was assigned to the 522nd Fighter-Bomber Squadron of the 27th Fighter-Bomber Group. The photograph was taken at Salerno, Italy, in 1943. (USAFM)

COCKPIT DETAILS

1. Cockpit Fluorescent Light
2. Windshield Defroster Control
3. Gun Sight
4. Ring and Bead Gun Sight (Stowed Position)
5. Windshield De-icer Spray Control
6. Cockpit Florescent Light
7. LH Gun Charging Handle
8. Magnetic Compass
9. Clock
10. Manifold Pressure Gage
12. RH Gun Charging Handle
13. Throttle
14. Accelerometer
15. Remote Contactor
16. Altimeter
17. Turn Indicator
18. Flight Indicator
19. Tachometer
20. Oxygen Flow Indicator
21. Enclosure Emergency Release Handle
22. Propeller Constant Speed Control
23. Landing Gear Emergency Down Control
24. Landing Gear Electrical Position Indicator
25. Air-speed Indicator
26. Bank and Turn Indicator
27. Rate-of-Climb Indicator
28. Coolant Temperature Indicator
29. Oil Temperature and Fuel and Oil Gage
30. Oxygen Flow Regulator

31. Carburetor Air Control
32. Contactor Heater Switch
33. Parking Brake Control Handle
34. Automatic Flare Discharger Control
35. Gun and Camera Safety Switch
36. Gun Heater Switch
37. Bomb Nose-Arming Switch
38. Bomb Tail-Arming Switch
39. Bomb Safety Switch
40. Propeller Selector Switch
41. Propeller Circuit Breaker Button
42. Oil Dilution Switch
43. Compass Light Switch and Rheostat Control
44. Cockpit Lights Switch and Rheostat Control
45. Engine Primer

46. Hydraulic Pressure Gage
47. Instrument Static Selector Valve
48. Bomb Control Handle
49. Ignition Switch
50. Starter Switch
51. Fuel Booster Pump Switch
52. Gun Sight Switch and Rheostat Control
53. LH Florescent Light Control
54. Landing Gear Control Handle
55. Leg-Length Adjustment Pins

56. Main Fuel System Selector Valve
57. Auxiliary Fuel System Selector Valve
58. Cockpit Cold-Air Ventilation Valve
59. Surface Control Lock
60. Hydraulic Hand Pump

The instrument panel in an A-36 is shown in this photograph that was taken from the flight manual. Keys for the numbered items are provided at right. **(USAFM)**

The left side of the cockpit is shown at left, while at right is a photograph of the right side. Keys for these two photographs are provided below except that numbers less than 61 are the same as the keys provided in the list above. **(USAFM)**

61. Recognition Light Keying Switch
62. Sliding Window Control
63. Spare Lamp Compartment
64. Pitot Heater Switch
65. White Recognition Light Switch
66. Red Recognition Light Switch
67. Green Recognition Light Switch
68. Amber Recognition Light Switch
69. Wing Navigation Light Switch
70. Tail Navigation Light Switch
71. RH Fluorescent Light Control
72. Landing Light Switch
73. Generator Disconnect Switch
74. Ammeter
75. Transmitter Key
76. Earphone Jack
77. Microphone Jack

78. Cockpit Light
79. Transmitter Light Selector Switch
80. Transmitter Power Toggle Switch
81. Transmitter Selector Switch
82. Jack Selector Switch, 3-6 MC
83. Receiver Signal Selector Switch, 3-6 MC
84. Jack Selector Switch, 190-550 KC
85. Receiver Signal Selector Switch, 190-550 KC
86. Jack Selector Switch, 6-9.1 MC
87. Receiver Signal Selector Switch, 6-9.1 MC
88. Receiver Volume Control, 3-6 MC
89. Receiver Frequency Control, 3-6 MC
90. Receiver Volume Control, 190-550 KC
91. Receiver Frequency Control, 190-550 KC
92. Receiver Volume Control 6-9.1 MC
93. Receiver Frequency Control, 6-9.1MC
94. Filter Switch Control

95. Right Fuel Tank Gage
96. Microphone Press-TO-Talk Switch
97. Mixture Control
98. Cockpit Light
99. Dive-Brake Control
100. Quadrant Friction Control
101. Flap Position Indicator
102. Radiator Air Scoop Position Indicator
103. Flap Control Handle
104. Radiator Air Scoop Control Handle
105. Rudder Trim Tab Control
106. Aileron Trim Tab Control
107. Landing Gear Mechanical Position Indicator
108. Bomb Control Antisalvo Guard
109. Tail Wheel Lock Control
110. Elevator Trim Tab Control

ARMAMENT

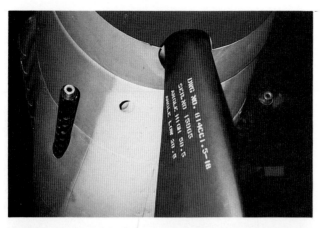 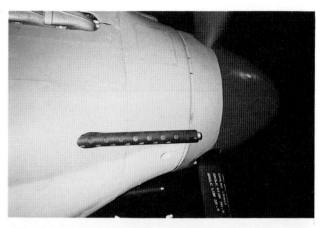

Details of the chin-mounted .50-caliber machine guns are shown in these two photographs. Note that there were no fairings where the barrels entered the fuselage as there were on the Mustang I. The Mustang I was the only other production variant to have these chin-mounted machine guns. The forward end of each gun is almost even with the rear of the spinner.

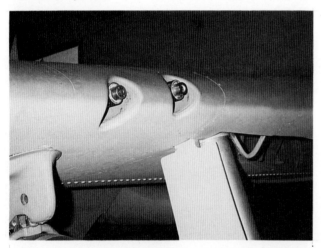 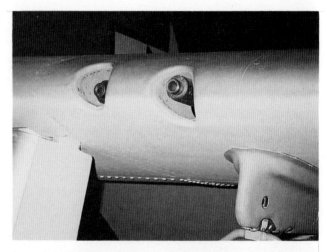

Four other .50-caliber machine guns were mounted in the wings. This wing armament was the same as found on all Mustang variants from the P-51 through the P-51C. The gun bays for the A-36 were the same as those shown for the P-51A on page 40. It should be noted that the guns were parallel to the ground rather than being in line with the dihedral of the wing. Therefore, the outer gun was mounted lower in the wing than the inner gun.

The A-36, along with the P-51A, were the first Mustangs to have under-wing pylons for carrying external stores. Bombs up to 500-pounds in weight could be carried on each pylon. Note the anti-sway braces, arming wires, and fuses on the bombs in these two photographs.

WING DETAILS

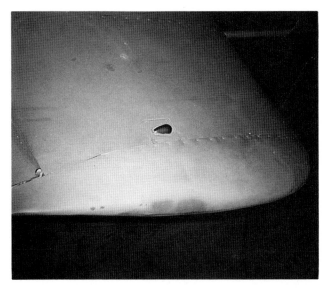 

Navigation lights were located on both the bottom and the top of each wing near the top. These teardrop-shaped lights were red on the left wing and green on the right wing. However, when not illuminated, the lens of the green lights appeared to be a dark blue color instead of green. At left is a photograph of the top light on the right wing, while at right is the red light on the top of the right wing.

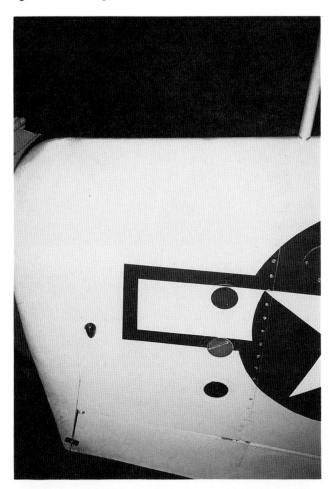

The light under the right wing tip can be seen here. Further inboard are the three larger round identification lights. They are flush with the underside of the wing and are red, amber, and green from front to rear. Again, the aft green light appears to be a dark blue when not illuminated.

The A-36 had a pitot boom mounted on the leading edge of the right wing near the tip. This was unique among Mustang variants. All other versions had the L-shaped pitot located under the right wing. This change was necessary on the A-36 because of the addition of the speed brakes.

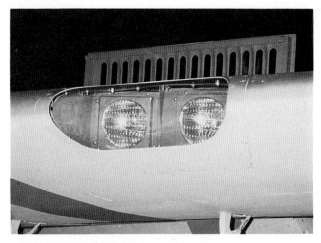

Another unique feature of the A-36 was the dual-lens landing/taxi light located in the leading edge of the left wing. The interior structure of the light was painted Chromate Green.

The trim tab on the left aileron can be seen here. The actuator is on the underside of the tab. The trim tab on the left aileron could be adjusted from the cockpit, but the one on the right aileron could only be adjusted on the ground.

This overall view shows the left flap in the lowered position. The part of the flap that would be hidden inside the wing when it was in the raised position remains unpainted.

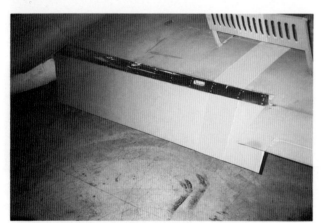

The right flap is illustrated here.

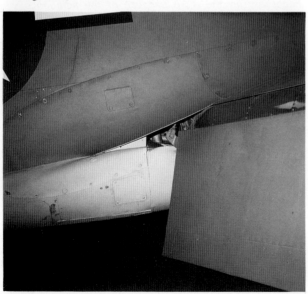

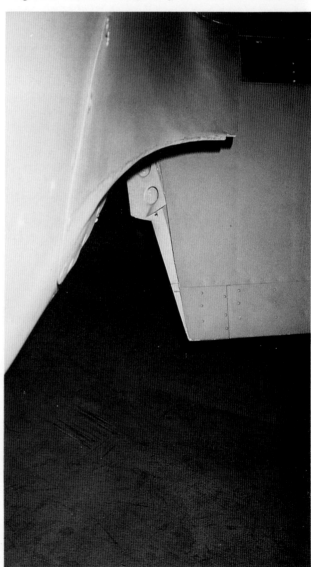

Details of where the right flap meets the fuselage can be seen in these two views. A fairing on the side of the fuselage overlaps the top of the flap at the inboard edge whenever the flap is closed.

DIVE BRAKE DETAILS

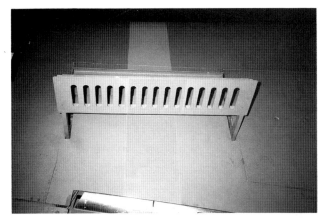

Dive brakes were fitted to the tops and bottoms of both wings. This is the top left brake as viewed from behind.

The bottom right brake can be seen here, and its well is also illustrated. The two bottom brakes were hinged at the front. This view provides a look at the angle of the brake when fully open.

The top right brake is shown here from the inside looking out toward the tip of the wing. The shallow well into which the brake fit when closed is also visible. Note that the two top brakes were hinged at the aft end.

The photograph at left shows the bottom left brake from behind. The actuating arms for the brake are clearly visible. At right is a similar view of the bottom right brake.

A-36

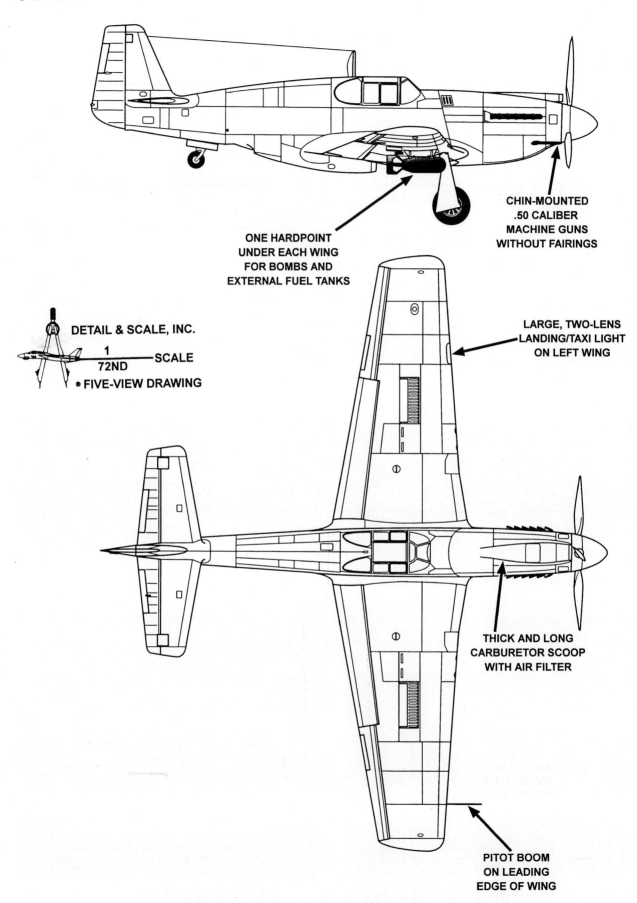

ONE HARDPOINT
UNDER EACH WING
FOR BOMBS AND
EXTERNAL FUEL TANKS

CHIN-MOUNTED
.50 CALIBER
MACHINE GUNS
WITHOUT FAIRINGS

DETAIL & SCALE, INC.

$\frac{1}{72ND}$ — SCALE

● FIVE-VIEW DRAWING

LARGE, TWO-LENS
LANDING/TAXI LIGHT
ON LEFT WING

THICK AND LONG
CARBURETOR SCOOP
WITH AIR FILTER

PITOT BOOM
ON LEADING
EDGE OF WING

DETAIL & SCALE, 1/72nd SCALE, COPYRIGHT DRAWING BY LLOYD JONES

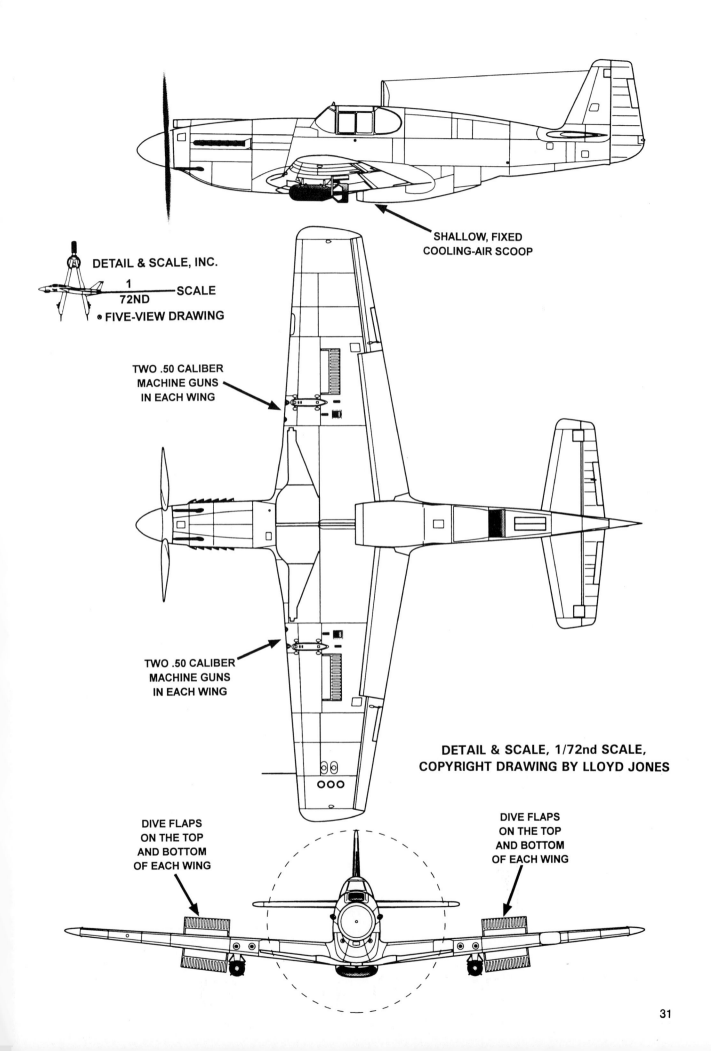

SHALLOW, FIXED
COOLING-AIR SCOOP

DETAIL & SCALE, INC.
$$\frac{1}{72ND}$$ SCALE
® FIVE-VIEW DRAWING

TWO .50 CALIBER
MACHINE GUNS
IN EACH WING

TWO .50 CALIBER
MACHINE GUNS
IN EACH WING

DETAIL & SCALE, 1/72nd SCALE,
COPYRIGHT DRAWING BY LLOYD JONES

DIVE FLAPS
ON THE TOP
AND BOTTOM
OF EACH WING

DIVE FLAPS
ON THE TOP
AND BOTTOM
OF EACH WING

DIMENSIONS

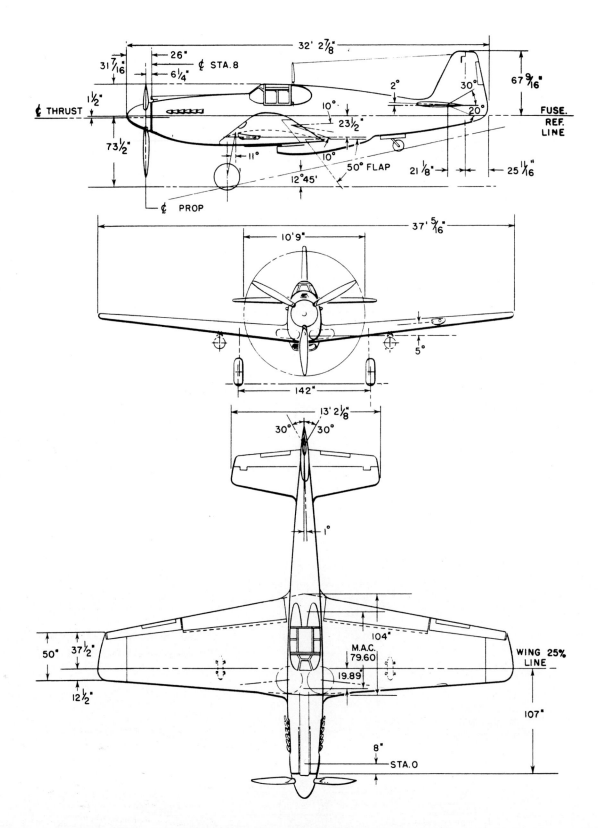

Taken from the A-36 erection and maintenance manual, this drawing shows the important dimensions for the aircraft. Except for the fact that this drawing shows the dual landing/taxi light of the A-36 and the under-wing pylons of the A-36 and the P-51A, it also applies to all Allison-powered, single-seat, variants of the Mustang. (USAFM)

COLOR GALLERY

Shown here with a tan and olive green camouflage scheme and with American national insignias, the first Mustang I of the second production batch can be identified by the British serial, AL958, painted on the side of its fuselage. The second production order of Mustang Is was given the North American model number NA-83, while the Mustang Is of the original order were North American model NA-73.   *(NAA via Ethell)*

This British Mustang IA has a circular section of its right rear cockpit window cut out to allow use of a camera mounted inside the rear cockpit area. This is unusual, because most camera installations were mounted on the left side. Removing the section of glass from the window was necessary in order to eliminate distortion from the photographs. Gray and green camouflage schemes were common on British Mustangs of all variants.   *(Astrella via Ethell)*

John P. "Jeep" Crowder flies an A-36A from the 524th Fighter Bomber Squadron past Mt. Etna, Sicily during 1943. The bars were added to the national insignia in June 1943, but unlike the bars which remain today, the red surround lasted only a short time. The unusual practice of putting two code letters in a vertical arrangement on the tail can be seen here.
(Crowder via Ethell)

Red and yellow spinners adorn A-36s assigned to a training unit in late 1943. The aircraft are painted in the standard Olive Drab over Neutral Gray scheme and have the red surround on the national insignias. Large aircraft numbers on the nose were standard for stateside training units.
(Ethell collection)

"Li'l Kitten" was a P-51B flown by Lt. Louis Fechet of the 357th Fighter Group. When Mustangs began to be delivered to operational squadrons in a natural metal finish, they were often painted by unit personnel. This was because many pilots did not think it was healthy to be flashing around the sky in a silver airplane. Standard U. S. colors were used on many occasions, but British paints were also seen on U. S. aircraft. If a camouflaged aircraft had its data block stencilled on a bare metal area as is the case here, it was a sure bet that the aircraft had been delivered without camouflage and was then painted in the field by unit personnel. To avoid having to restencil the entire data block, the stencilling was masked off, then the rest of the aircraft was painted. (Astrella via Ethell)

"Snoots Sniper" was assigned to the 352nd Fighter Group and flown by Lt. Francis Horne who was credited with five and one-half victories. The Mustang was named for the crew chief, Art "Snoots" Snyder.
(Astrella via Ethell)

The WW on the vertical tail of this Mustang stands for "War Weary." Such aircraft, which were no longer able to stand the rigors of combat, were often transformed into hack aircraft by operational units. The fuselage fuel tank was removed and replaced with a second seat. The spine was modified to take a second canopy. This aircraft was flown by the 355th Fighter Squadron of the 354th Fighter Group. (Riche via Ethell)

P-51A COCKPIT DETAILS & COLORS

The photographs on this and the next page were taken in the cockpit of a restored P-51A Mustang at the Yanks Air Museum in Chino, California. It has been restored according to original specifications as much as possible while still allowing the aircraft to be flown today. This is the main instrument panel in the P-51A which was very similar to that in the A-36 as well as the P-51B/C which followed.

The basic layout and the equipment on the left side of the cockpit remained very similar in all versions of the Mustang.

Details on the right side of the P-51A's cockpit are seen here. Note the wooden case for the airplane's flight records.

The floor in the cockpit of Allison-powered Mustangs was simply the top of the metal wing structure. On Merlin-powered variants, a wooden floor was placed above the wing structure. The cold air vent is located to the left of the control column.

Above: Details of the seat back, the armor plate behind the pilot's head, and the shoulder harness are illustrated here.

Right: The seat bucket and seat belts can be seen in this photo. Also note the gage for the right fuel tank on the floor of the cockpit.

The base of the control column can be seen here. Note the gage for the left fuel tank on the floor next to the corner of the seat. The hot air vent and controls are to the right of the control column.

ALLISON ENGINE DETAILS & COLORS

With the panels on the right side removed, details of the Allison V-1710-81 engine in a P-51A can be see here.

This photograph shows the left side of the Allison engine.

Here is a view from underneath the engine looking aft. Chromate Yellow primer was used on the interior framework.

These two views show the engine accessory compartment between the firewall and the aft end of the engine block. The photograph at left was taken from the right side, while the one at right was taken from the left side of the aircraft.

MERLIN ENGINE DETAILS & COLORS

Bill Gertzen, the crew chief on Lt. Robert Woody's P-51B, performs maintenance on the fighter's Merlin engine. This aircraft was assigned to the 355th Fighter Group. The colors of the engine, oil tank, and framework of an actual P-51B during World War II are visible in this rare color photograph of maintenance activities. Note also how dark the Neutral Gray appears. This is a correct value for this color which is often mistakenly thought to be lighter than it actually was.
(Ethell collection)

The entire nose section was a single sub-assembly that could be removed and shipped with the Merlin engine installed in it. Both sides of this complete assembly are illustrated in these two photographs. Note the metal shroud around the exhausts. This shroud was on most Merlin-powered Mustangs.

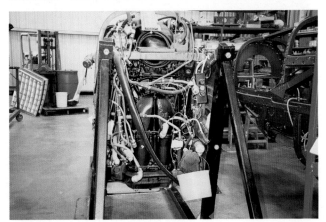

At left is a look at the aft end of the Merlin engine installed in the nose section. At right is a photograph of the forward fuselage without the engine installed. The oil tank can be seen mounted to the firewall, and the design of the framework is visible.

GUN BAY DETAILS & COLORS

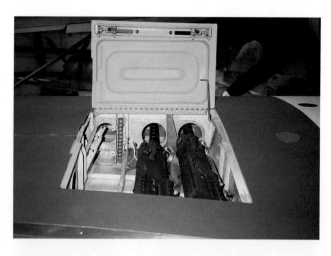 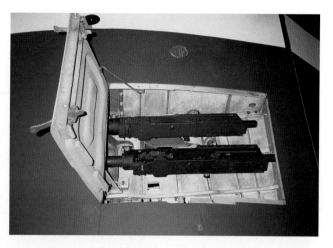

With the exception of the Mustang I, all production variants of the Mustang up through the P-51B and -C had four .50-caliber machine guns in the wings. Although there was room for three guns in each bay, only two were installed. They were mounted in pairs and were tilted at an angle with the inboard weapon being positioned a little further forward than the outboard. The tilting resulted in jamming problems, and as a result, the machine guns in the P-51D and subsequent versions were mounted upright. A third gun was also installed in each bay beginning with the -D. At left is the left gun bay from behind, while at right is the same bay looking inboard. Note that the inside of the door is painted Chromate Yellow. On production aircraft, the interior of the bay would have also been painted with this primer as well, instead of being left natural metal.

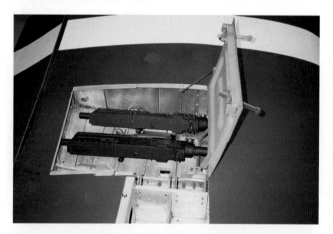 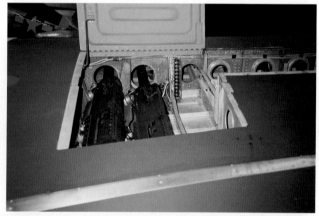

These two photographs show the right gun bay. The feed chutes and the ammunition have been removed, but they would look the same as in the photographs and keys from the manual shown on page 61.

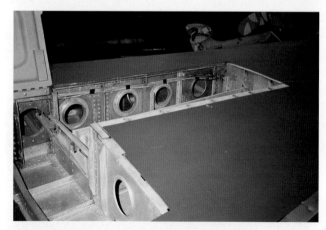 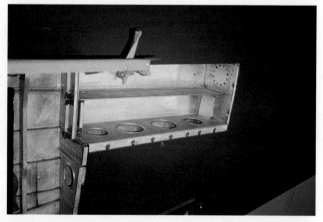

The ammunition was contained in a divided area outboard of the guns. Ammunition in the forward section supplied the inboard gun, while the outboard gun was fed ammunition from the aft section of this area. At left is the ammunition storage area for the right wing guns on a P-51A as seen from above, while at right is the same area viewed from behind. Note the lightening holes around this area.

P-51A & MUSTANG II

Although most P-51As were painted Olive Drab over Neutral Gray, this aircraft remains in a natural metal finish. It is a P-51A-10-NA, which was the last production block for the -A variant.　　　*(Gordon Williams via Jones)*

The P-51A was essentially an A-36 without the dive-bombing equipment. Like the A-36, it had a fixed cooling-air scoop for the radiator. But the L-shaped pitot probe was mounted under the wing as it was on all fighter versions of the Mustang. There was only one landing/taxi light instead of the dual unit found on the A-36. To give the P-51A better performance at higher altitudes the Allison V-1710-81 engine was installed. It had a better supercharger, but it still could not match the performance of the supercharger used with the V-1710 in the P-38 or the subsequent Merlin engine. Like the A-36, the P-51A had the air filter in the carburetor scoop, thus causing it to

be the wider design.

To make the aircraft lighter, the two chin-mounted guns were deleted, leaving the P-51A with four .50-caliber machine guns in the wings. A total of 1,260 rounds of ammunition was carried for these weapons. Like the A-36, the P-51A was fitted with two under-wing pylons which could each carry a bomb up to the 500-pound size. But in the case of the P-51A, these stations were normally used to carry external fuel tanks. In a few cases P-51As were fitted with triple rocket tubes.

Originally, 1200 P-51As were ordered, but this number was reduced to 310 in December 1942. During

The very first P-51A-1-NA was one of two flown to Ladd Field in Alaska for testing with skis in place of the standard landing gear. Even with the skis, the landing gear could be retracted.
(USAFM)

P-51A & MUSTANG II

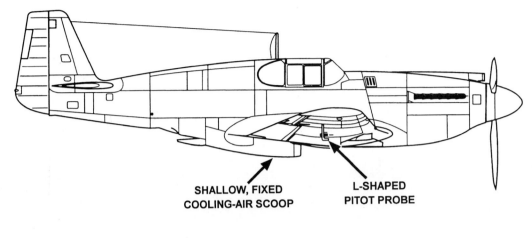

SHALLOW, FIXED
COOLING-AIR SCOOP

L-SHAPED
PITOT PROBE

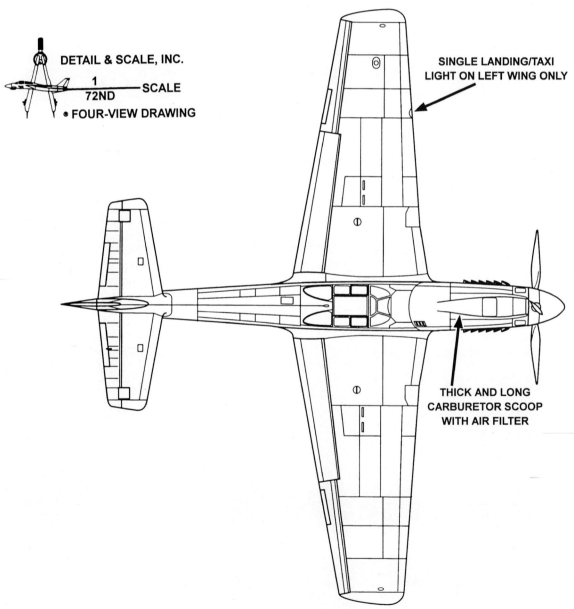

DETAIL & SCALE, INC.

$\dfrac{1}{72\text{ND}}$ — SCALE

● FOUR-VIEW DRAWING

SINGLE LANDING/TAXI
LIGHT ON LEFT WING ONLY

THICK AND LONG
CARBURETOR SCOOP
WITH AIR FILTER

DETAIL & SCALE, 1/72nd SCALE, COPYRIGHT DRAWING BY LLOYD JONES

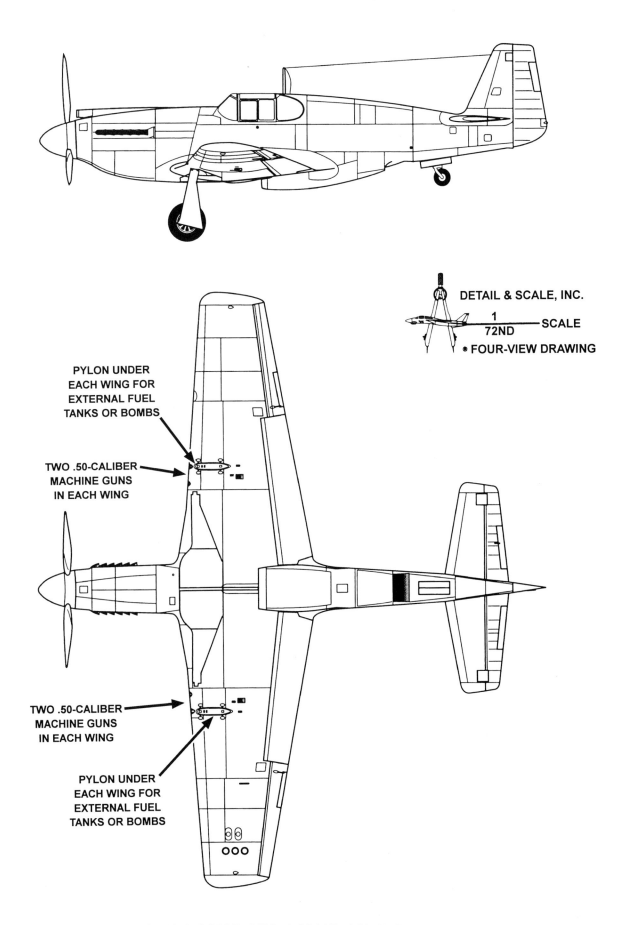

PYLON UNDER
EACH WING FOR
EXTERNAL FUEL
TANKS OR BOMBS

TWO .50-CALIBER
MACHINE GUNS
IN EACH WING

DETAIL & SCALE, INC.

$\dfrac{1}{72\text{ND}}$ —— SCALE

⊛ FOUR-VIEW DRAWING

TWO .50-CALIBER
MACHINE GUNS
IN EACH WING

PYLON UNDER
EACH WING FOR
EXTERNAL FUEL
TANKS OR BOMBS

DETAIL & SCALE, 1/72nd SCALE, COPYRIGHT DRAWING BY LLOYD JONES

The major internal components of the P-51A are visible in this general arrangement illustration. *(USAFM)*

"Slick Chick" was the second P-51A built, and it was used for tests and evaluations at Wright Field. Most P-51As had a small window on the left side of the windscreen as is the case on this aircraft. *(USAFM)*

the previous month, the first XP-51B had flown with the Merlin engine, and the USAAF opted to buy this new high-altitude version instead. There were already plenty of P-39s and P-40s on hand to handle the low-level chores.

Fifty P-51As were sent to the Royal Air Force where they received the Mustang II designation. Thirty-five of the American aircraft were fitted with cameras and

designated F-6Bs.

The first unit to take the P-51A into combat was the 311th Fighter Bomber Group based in India. This group also flew the A-36, and the use of two very similar aircraft simplified operations, maintenance, and logistics. Other units to operate the type were the Flying Tigers of the 23rd Fighter Group and the 1st Air Commando Group.

Thirty-five P-51As were fitted with cameras in the rear section of the cockpit. These photo-reconnaissance aircraft were designated F-6Bs. In the example illustrated here, the camera is small enough to fit inside the standard window. However, there was usually a small circle cut from the glass to prevent distortion in the photographs.

LANDING GEAR DETAILS

Above left and right: Details of the strut, tire, wheel, and outer door of the left main landing gear on a P-51A can be seen in these two views. The strut and wheel are flat silver, and the interior of the door is chromate green. The landing gear illustrated on this and the next two pages was standard on Mustangs up through the P-51B/C. Beginning with the P-51D, some detail changes were made to the main landing gear, although the basic design remained the same.

The inner left landing gear door is shown here. The section in the center part of the door was often left unpainted, but the rest of the door is Chromate Green. The interior portion of the gear well is also visible.

This is the outer part of the left main gear well.

The spoke pattern on the wheel can be seen in this view of the right main landing gear.

More details of the right main landing gear are shown here. Again, this was essentially the same on all Mustangs up through the P-51C.

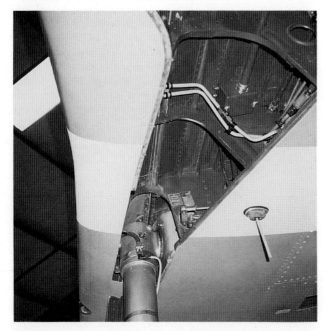

This view looks up and out into the right main gear well. Note the point where the strut joins with the wing structure.

Details of the inner part of the right main gear are visible in this photograph. Note the relationship of the leading edge of the wing to the front of the well.

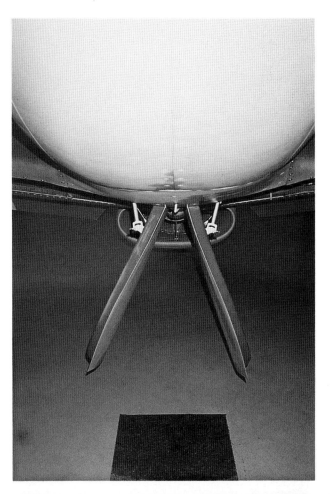

Above: The shape of the inner main gear doors remained essentially the same on Mustangs up through the P-51C. But when the wing was redesigned for the P-51D, the shape of these doors also changed.

Right: The correct angle for the inner doors in the fully open position is illustrated here. When the aircraft was shut down, hydraulic pressure held these doors closed for a while. But as the pressure bled off, the doors gradually dropped to this position.

Above left: The tail gear is shown here from the right side. However, because the aircraft was pushed back to its parked position, the wheel castored around. Therefore this is actually the left side of the wheel and tire.

Above right: The right side of the tail wheel, strut, and tire are visible here, although this photograph was taken from the left side of the aircraft.

Left: This close-up was taken from directly behind the tail wheel. It shows the top of the strut, and the rods which close the two tail wheel doors when the gear is retracted. Note the correct angle of the doors in the open position. They are not vertical as might be expected.

CANOPY DETAILS

Except for those fitted with a Malcolm hood, the standard canopy enclosure for all Mustang variants up through the P-51C remained essentially the same. These two views show the standard flush canopy from both sides.

Details of the windscreen are illustrated here. On most P-51As, there was a small window that could be opened on the left side panel. However, it is not present on this particular aircraft.

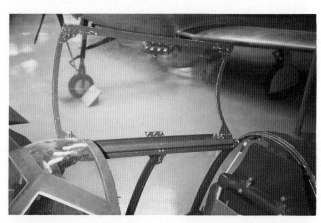

The top part of the canopy hinged open from the right side to make ingress and egress easier. The interior of the canopy's framework was painted Chromate Green.

The right side of the canopy was fixed, but the forward portion was a window that slid aft as illustrated here. The handle for moving and locking the window in place can be seen at the bottom a few inches from the leading edge.

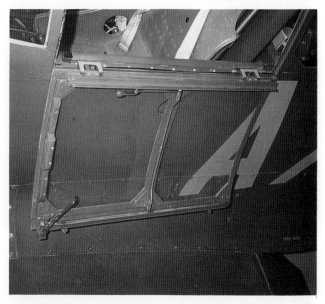

The left side window was hinged at the bottom, and it opened against the side of the fuselage. Note the red handle at the corner of the window.

NOSE DETAILS

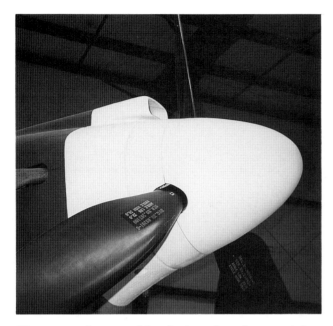 

These two views provide a look at the spinner and the carburetor scoop on top of the nose. Note that the spinner is split into forward and aft parts where the propeller blades enter. A small hinged panel, visible in the photograph at right, was where the glycol coolant was added.

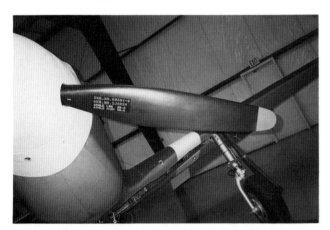 

Allison-powered Mustangs were fitted with a three-blade Curtiss Electric propeller. The stenciling on one of the blades is visible in this view.

Each blade had the outer five inches of the tip painted yellow. On the back of each blade was a small yellow line used when calibrating the pitch of the propeller.

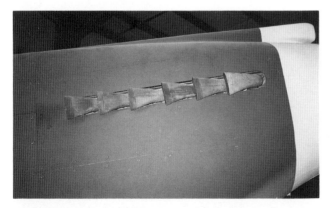 

Allison-powered Mustangs had six exhaust ports on each side, and these were almost always the flat "fish-tailed" design shown in these two photographs. The Allison engine produced a lot of rich exhaust at times, and as a result, the sides of the fuselage around and just aft of these exhausts were often very stained with black and gray smudges and discoloration. It should also be noted that the panel lines around these exhausts and the Allison engine were quite different than those found on the later Merlin-powered aircraft.

FUSELAGE DETAILS

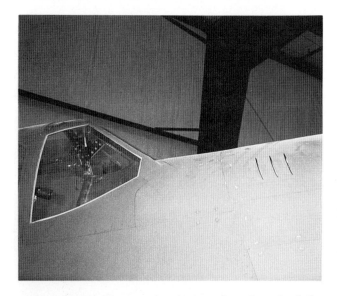

Three small vents were located at the aft end of the engine compartment on the right side of the P-51A and the other Allison-powered Mustangs.

The oil filler was on the top left side of the fuselage, just forward of the windscreen.

This is the top cover for the engine accessory compartment after being removed from the aircraft. Both the vents and the access door for the oil filler can be seen on this piece of the aircraft's skin. The engine accessory compartment is illustrated on page 38.

A flare pistol, which was carried inside the cockpit, could be fired through a hole in the left side of the fuselage. An exterior view of the hole is provided at left, while at right is the port inside the cockpit through which the pistol was fired.

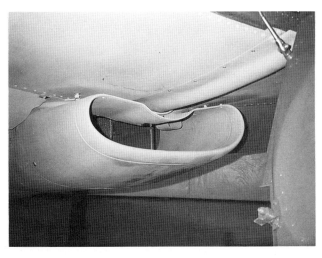 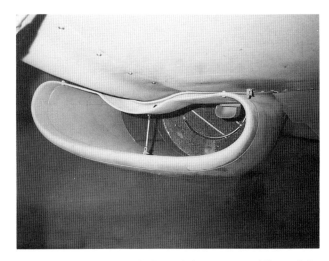

The P-51A had the shallow fixed cooling-air intake for the radiator. At left is a general view of the scoop, while at right is a close up looking down the intake to the front of the radiator. This same scoop was also used on the A-36.

The hot air exit ramp is shown here from the left rear. Note the tapered shape of the side of the ramp. The hot air exiting this ramp produced enough thrust to more than make up for the drag caused by the cooling-air scoop.

The aft end of the radiator is visible in this photograph as is the interior of the exit ramp and ducting.

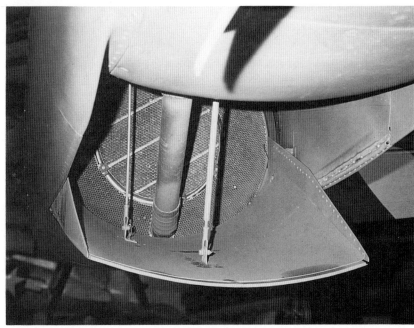

WING DETAILS

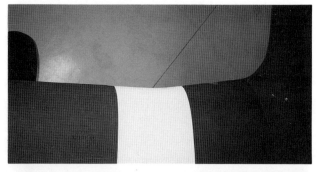

Although there were some minor detail differences, the planform of the wing used on all Mustangs up through the P-51B/C was basically the same. On the P-51D, a fillet would be added to the leading edge at the root, but as clearly illustrated in the top view shown at left, there was only a very small change in the angle of the leading edge on the earlier versions. This is the leading edge of the left wing. At right is a front view of the same leading edge showing the gun camera installation.

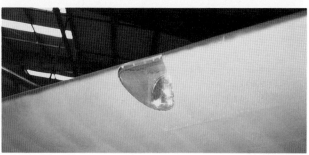

The P-51A retained the four .50-caliber wing guns as used on the P-51, A-36, and the subsequent P-51B and P-51C. Again, note how the guns are mounted level to the ground rather than to the dihedral of the wing. These are the guns on the right wing.

Although the P-51 had a single-lens landing/taxi light on each wing, and the A-36 had a dual-lens light on the left wing, the P-51A had only a single light on the left wing. This feature remained the same on the P-51B and P-51C as well.

Navigation lights on the P-51A remained the same teardrop-shaped fixtures on the top and bottom of each wing near the tip. At right is the top light on the right wing, and at left is the lower light on the underside of the left wing. This feature remained the same for all Mustangs until it was replaced with a single light on the tip of each wing on the P-51D.

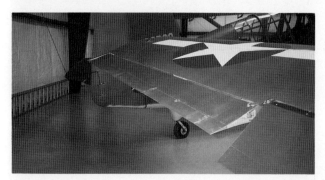

The ailerons on the P-51A were the same as on earlier Mustangs. During the production of the P-51B, two small fairings were installed on the top of the wing just forward of the aileron, while a single fairing was located on the underside. (See page 60.) As can be seen here, these fairings were not on the P-51A, nor were they on any of the earlier variants.

The underside of the ailerons and flaps are illustrated in these two views. Note the actuators for the trim tabs on each aileron. Only the left aileron trim tab could be adjusted from the cockpit.

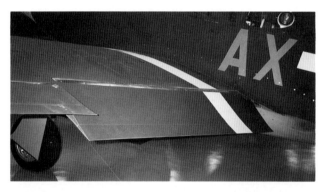

This is the top of the left flap, and it is slightly lowered. The natural metal leading edge of the flap is visible where it meets the wing. This natural metal is completely covered when the flap is in the full up position.

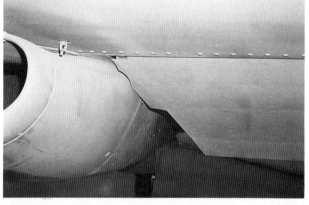

Note the irregular shape of the inboard edge of the flap where it meets the fuselage.

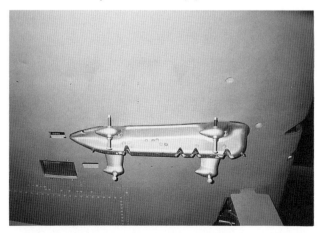

Like the A-36, the P-51A had under-wing pylons for carrying external stores. But in the case of the P-51A, these were used more often for carrying external fuel tanks than bombs. Also note the shell and link ejection holes in the underside of the wing.

This L-shaped pitot was standard on all versions of the Mustang except the A-36. It was located under the right wing.

TAIL DETAILS

The design of the Mustang's tail changed very little from variant to variant until the "tall-tailed" P-51H was introduced. In the photograph at left, note that the actuator for the trim tab on the rudder is on the right side at the bottom of the tab. There is a white position light near the bottom of the rudder's trailing edge.

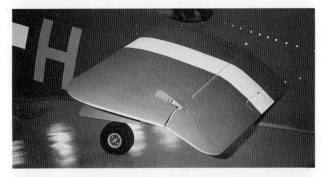 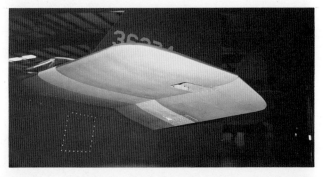

Details of the left horizontal stabilizer and elevator are shown in these two views. Note that the actuator for the trim tab on this side is on the underside as seen in the photo at right.

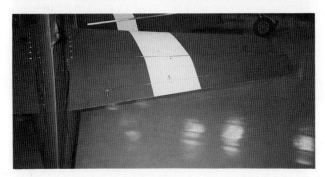 

At left is a look at the underside of the right horizontal stabilizer and elevator, and at right is a top view. Note that the actuator for the trim tab is on the top for this side. Also notice the rather sizable gap between the elevator and the vertical tail.

XP-51B

The first of two XP-51Bs is shown here. It carried no armament.
(USAFM)

The second XP-51B retained the four 20-mm cannon as used on the P-51. Both of the XP-51Bs were converted from standard P-51s.   *(USAFM)*

In mid-1941, during production of the P-51, the 93rd and 102nd airframe off the line were reserved for test purposes with the Packard Merlin engine. This was a license-built U. S. version of the excellent Rolls Royce Merlin being produced in England. Concurrently, the British were fitting test aircraft with Rolls Royce 65 engines and four-bladed propellers like those used on some Spitfire variants. In England, these were given the Mustang X designation. The USAAF chose the four-bladed Hamilton-Standard 24D50-65 cuffed propeller for use with the Packard Merlin.

The fact that the USAAF identified these two P-51s for testing with the Merlin engine before the Japanese attack on Pearl Harbor, and even before the first test flight of either XP-51, is testimony to two important historical points. First, the USAAF did in fact have a genuine interest in the new airplane, and to the best of its ability within funding constraints, was planning ahead for the future. Second, it was already understood that the Allison engine would produce excellent low-altitude fighters, but a different powerplant and supercharger combination would be necessary for high-altitude variants.

One of the two XP-51Bs was left without armament, while the second retained the standard P-51 armament consisting of four 20-mm cannon. The first flight of an XP-51B took place on 30 November, 1942, shortly after the Mustang X flew in England. On both sides of the Atlantic, the first high-altitude version of the Mustang was born.

Cockpit details in one of the XP-51Bs are illustrated in this photograph.   *(USAFM)*

This is the Merlin engine installation in one of the XP-51Bs.   *(NAA via Olmstead)*

P-51B, P-51C, & MUSTANG III

The first production P-51B was 43-12093. The three-bladed Curtiss Electric propeller, used with the Allison-powered Mustangs, was replaced with a four-bladed Hamilton Standard propeller. **(NAA via Jones)**

The first production P-51B took to the air on its maiden flight on 5 May, 1943. North American's plant in California would follow it with almost 2,000 more examples. But even this was not enough. In Dallas, North American open a second production line producing identical copies designated P-51Cs. Total production in Texas would provide another 1,750 Mustangs for the war effort.

The Packard Merlin V-1650-3 was used on the first production machines, but this was changed to the V-1650-7 beginning with the P-51B-10-NA and the P-51C-5-

5-NT. Equipped with a 2-speed, 2-stage supercharger designed by Wright, it was an outstanding powerplant that gave the Mustang performance that matched or bettered the top propeller-driven fighters of the Luftwaffe at high altitudes. Although performance was adequate below 15,000 feet, the Allison-powered versions actually performed better at these lower altitudes.

In November 1943, when the 354th Fighter Group became the first to receive the new Mustang, the concept of using unescorted bombers on daylight raids had proven unwise to say the least. Although the P-38

This P-51B is from the 336th Fighter Squadron of the 4th Fighter Group. "This one's for Harry," is written on the 500-pound bomb carried beneath the left wing. Note how the Malcolm canopy slid aft, thus necessitating the removal of the radio mast. The mast was usually replaced by a whip antenna mounted further aft on the spine.
(Roeder collection)

This particular P-51B has both the Malcolm hood and the ventral strake on the aft spine of the aircraft. Although this strake was eventually added to almost all P-51Ds, it was relatively rare on P-51Bs and P-51Cs. The 7F fuselage code belongs to the 485th Fighter Squadron of the 370th Fighter Group. **(USAFM)**

The ventral strake can be seen again on P-51C-11-NO, 44-10790. Also note the loop antenna on the spine of the aircraft. This photograph was taken in Burma during August 1944. The checks on the tail are yellow and black. (Ethell collection)

had been available from the beginning as a long-range escort fighter with high-altitude capability, many had been sent outside the European Theater of Operations. Some had gone to Africa, while others continued to prove their capabilities as a long range fighter over the wide expanses of the Pacific Ocean. When the decision was made to provide escort for the heavy bombers in Europe, the USAAF not only needed good escort fighters, it needed lots of them. That is what the production lines in California and Texas could provide.

Most of the visible changes made to the Mustang's airframe to build the P-51B and P-51C were directly related to the engine change. The carburetor scoop was moved from on top of the nose to a position below it. The forward end of this larger scoop was just aft of the spinner. The cooling-air scoop under the fuselage was enlarged. As viewed from the side, the lip for the scoop was cut at an angle rather than being even as on the Allison-powered versions. The entire inlet was positioned further away from the bottom of the fuselage and wing. Almost every other feature remained the same. The single landing/taxi light was retained in the leading edge of the left wing. As it had been with the P-51A, armament was four .50-caliber machine guns, all of which were located in the wings. Seventy-one camera-equipped P-51Bs were designated F-6C-NAs while twenty P-51Cs fitted with the same camera installations were officially labeled F-6C-NTs.

It has been claimed that the Merlin engine was more fuel efficient than the Allison, but figures and charts do not show this to be the case. For example, configured for long range escort, a P-51A with 480 gallons of gas could fly 2550 miles. Similarly configured, a P-51B with 489 gallons could reach 2080 miles. Depending on the altitude flown, combat loadings, and other factors, these figures varied. Under certain conditions the Allison provided longer legs, but in other situations, the Merlin ranged farther. The simple fact is that either engine could provide considerable range.

To increase range even more, an 85-gallon fuel tank was installed in the fuselage behind the cockpit. This was added to the production lines with the P-51B-10-NA and the P-51C-5-NT. The tank was also retrofitted to some existing P-51Bs and -Cs.

The addition of the fuselage fuel tank produced almost disastrous results. When fully fueled, the center of gravity of the aircraft was moved beyond the point of danger. As a result, the practice was to limit the amount of fuel in this tank to only sixty-five gallons. Even so, it was difficult, if not impossible, to lift the tail wheel off of the runway during take-offs. Pilots would lift the main gear off first, then wait until sufficient speed was reached to fly the tail off. An engine failure during this take-off would spell disaster.

But there was a further problem with the fuselage tank as well. Normal procedure would be to burn off the external fuel tanks first, then drop the empties in the event of combat. But this would often leave considerable fuel in the fuselage tank, and if so, any combat maneuvering could throw the Mustang and even the best pilot wildly out of control. The alternative was to burn off the fuel in the fuselage tank first so that the center of gravity would be where it was supposed to be. But the sixty-five gallons in that tank would put the aircraft well over enemy territory, and very often, pilots found themselves punching off full external tanks. It was a no-win situation.

To remind the pilot of this potentially dangerous situation, a white or black + was painted on the side of the fuselage near the data block on aircraft with the fuselage tank. The center-of-gravity problem with the fuselage tank continued with the P-51D and P-51K versions and was not corrected until the P-51H which had a redesigned fuselage.

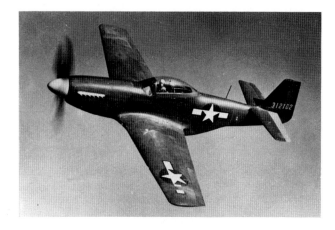

P-51B-1-NA, 43-12102, became the test aircraft for what would become the P-51D. The spine was cut down, and a full bubble canopy was fitted. Note that the wing on this aircraft remained the same as used on the P-51B and earlier Mustangs rather than being replaced with the redesigned wing of the P-51D. (USAFM)

COCKPIT DETAILS

Details of the instrument panel in a P-51B are indicated in this photograph and the keys below. *(USAFM)*

1. Crash Pad
2. Gun Sight
3. Clock
4. Fluorescent Light
5. Compass
6. Directional Gyro
7. Remote Contactor
8. Altimeter
9. Boost Control
10. Landing Gear Position Indicator
11. Airspeed Indicator
12. Control Stick
13. Armament Control Panel
14. Bank-and-Turn Indicator
15. Parking Brake Handle
16. Booster Pump Switches
17. Ignition Switch
18. Fuel Selector Valve Control
19. Supercharger Control Switch
20. Left-hand Fluorescent Light Switch

Features of the optical gun sight and the auxiliary ring and bead sight are identified here. *(USAFM)*

1. AUXILIARY RING SIGHT SOCKET
2. ARMOR PLATE GLASS WINDSHIELD
3. SUN FILTER
4. REFLECTOR
5. CRASH PAD
6. CRASH PAD STRAP
7. VERTICAL ADJUSTMENT BOLTS
8. GUNSIGHT HOUSING
9. SPRING-LOADED PLUNGER
10. AUXILIARY RING SIGHT
11. REFLECTOR ASSEMBLY LOCKSCREW
12. RETICLE ADJUSTMENT KNOB
13. MIRROR ACCESS COVER PLATE
14. AUXILIARY RING SIGHT STOWAGE CLIPS

21. Emergency Fairing Door Control
22. Hydraulic Pressure Gage
23. Compass Light Switch
24. Gun Sight Rheostat
25. Starter Switch
26. Oil Dilution Switch
27. Supercharger Warning Light
28. Engine Primer
29. Oxygen Pressure Gage
30. Oxygen System Warning Light
31. Rate-of-Climb Indicator
32. Coolant Temperature Indicator
33. Oil Temperature and Fuel and Oil Pressure Gage
34. Tachometer
35. Oxygen Flow Blinker
36. Flight Indicator
37. Manifold Pressure Gage
38. Suction Gage
39. Fluorescent Light

Details of the left side of the cockpit are illustrated in the photograph at left, and the right side of the cockpit is shown in the photo at right. Keys for the callouts in both pictures are provided below. *(USAFM)*

40. Card Holder
41. Throttle
42. Throat Microphone Switch
43. Propeller Control
44. Mixture Control
45. Quadrant Friction Lock
46. Aileron Trim Tab Control
47. Oil Cooler Exit Flap Control
48. Coolant Radiator Exit Flap Control
49. Sliding Window Handle
50. Cockpit Light
51. Signal Pistol Holder
52. Wing Flap Control
53. Carburetor Air Control
54. Rudder Trim Tab Control
55. Elevator Trim Tab Control
56. Left Fuel Tank Gage
57. Windshield Defroster Control
58. Landing Gear Control
59. Bomb Control Handle
60. Bomb Antisalvo Guard
61. Map Case
62. SCR-535-A Radio Control Box
63. SCR-522-A Radio Control Box
64. Sliding Window Handle
65. Airplane Restriction Plate
66. Ammeter
67. Position Light Switches
68. Landing Light Switch
69. Pitot Heater Switch
70. Battery-disconnect Switch
71. Generator-disconnect Switch
72. Right-hand Fluorescent Light Switch
73. Oxygen Regulator
74. Enclosure Emergency Release handle
75. Spare Lamp Stowage
76. Circuit-breaker Buttons
77. Hydraulic Hand-pump
78. Cockpit Light
79. Right Fuel Tank Gage
80. Detonator Switches
81. Hot Air Control
82. Relief Tube

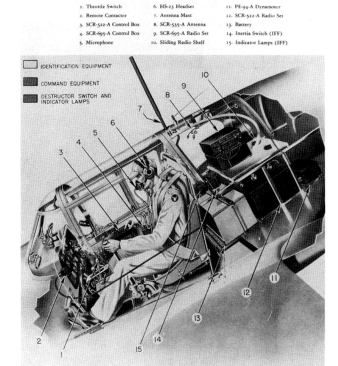

Early P-51Bs and P-51Cs were originally built without a fuselage fuel tank. Beginning with production blocks P-51B-10-NA and P-51C-5-NT, an 85-gallon fuel tank was added in the fuselage just aft of the pilot. Fuselage tanks were also retrofitted to some of the early production P-51Bs and P-51Cs that had been originally built without them. The addition of the tank necessitated a change in the type of radio gear installed and its location. The photograph at left identifies the equipment installed in those aircraft without the fuselage tank, while at right is the equipment used after the tank was installed. The tank adversely and dangerously affected the center of gravity of the aircraft, so a + was stencilled on the side of the fuselage near the data block to alert the pilot that the tank was installed. In practice, only sixty-five gallons were carried in the tank to prevent the Mustang from being too far out of balance. (Both USAFM)

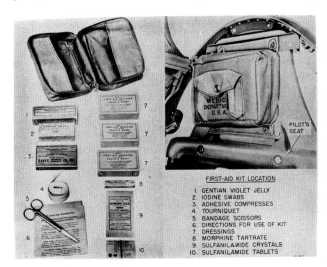

FIRST-AID KIT LOCATION

1. GENTIAN VIOLET JELLY
2. IODINE SWABS
3. ADHESIVE COMPRESSES
4. TOURNIQUET
5. BANDAGE SCISSORS
6. DIRECTIONS FOR USE OF KIT
7. DRESSINGS
8. MORPHINE TARTRATE
9. SULFANILAMIDE CRYSTALS
10. SULFANILAMIDE TABLETS

Above: A first-aid kit was located behind the pilot's head. The contents of the kit are identified in this photograph from the flight manual. (USAFM)

Right: Details of the seat are identified in this drawing from the P-51B/C erection and maintenance manual. (USAFM)

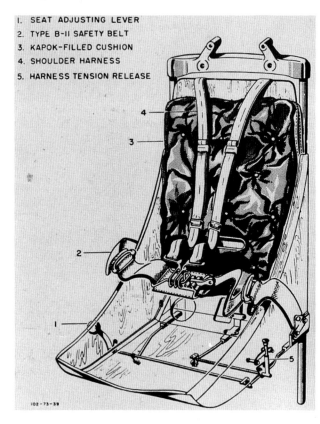

1. SEAT ADJUSTING LEVER
2. TYPE B-11 SAFETY BELT
3. KAPOK-FILLED CUSHION
4. SHOULDER HARNESS
5. HARNESS TENSION RELEASE

102-73-39

On Merlin-powered Mustangs, to include the P-51B and P-51C, a wood floor was added inside the cockpit. The photo at left shows how the floor surrounded the control column and the center console below the instrument panel. The knob to the left of the column is the control for defroster air. The one to the right is the hot air control. Fuel gages were still mounted on the top of the wing, but they were visible through holes at the aft end of the wooden floor. The gage for the right wing tank can be seen in the close-up at right. The gage for the left wing was the same on the other side. The floor came from the factory with a clear sealant on the plywood, but the wood was often stained or painted in the field. Evidence indicates that when the floor was painted, flat black was the color used most often. Forward is to the top of these photographs.

P-51B/C DETAIL DIFFERENCES

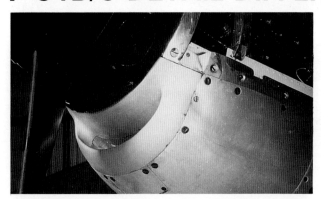
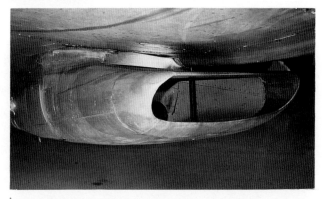

Compared to the P-51A, the most noticeable differences on the P-51B and P-51C were related to the engine change. The carburetor intake scoop was moved from the top of the nose to a position under the spinner as shown at left. The cooling-air intake under the fuselage was much deeper, and there was a larger gap between it and the bottom of the wing as seen in the photograph at right. The lip of the intake was angled, while it was even on the earlier variants.

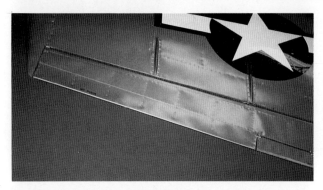
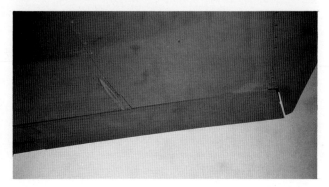

The wing on the P-51B and P-51C was originally the same as that on the P-51A. During the production run of the P-51B/C, two small aerodynamic fairings were added to the top of each wing just forward of the ailerons. The fairings on the left wing can be seen in the photograph at left. On the underside of the wing, only one fairing was added. It was directly opposite the outboard fairing on the top of the wing. The fairing under the left wing can be seen at right. This change was made to the wing early in the production of P-51Bs and P-51Cs, and the fairings were retrofitted to aircraft originally produced without them.

GUN ARMAMENT

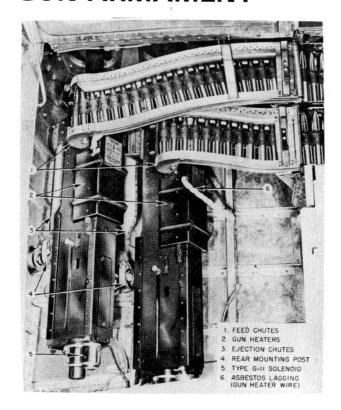

1. FEED CHUTES
2. GUN HEATERS
3. EJECTION CHUTES
4. REAR MOUNTING POST
5. TYPE G-11 SOLENOID
6. ASBESTOS LAGGING (GUN HEATER WIRE)

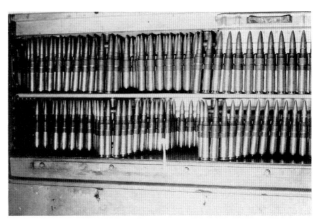

Above left and right: The installation of four .50-caliber machine guns in the wings of the P-51B/C remained the same as it had on the P-51, P-51A, and A-36. These two photographs show the installation in the right wing. The arrangement in the left wing was simply a mirror image of what is shown here. The guns were installed at a tilted angle, which made them subject to jamming. Note that there is room for a third gun in the bay, although it was never installed until the production of the P-51D. Ammunition was stored in a divided compartment just outboard of the guns as seen above. (Both USAFM)

P-51B, P-51C, & MUSTANG III

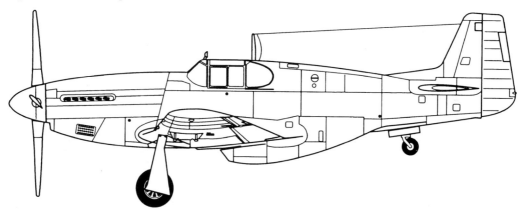

P-51B/-C WITH DORSAL FIN

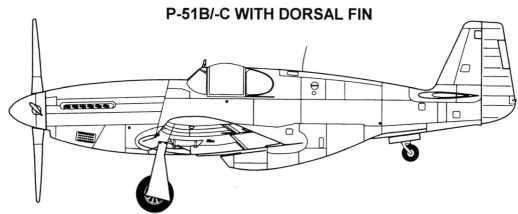

P-51B/-C WITH MALCOLM CANOPY

DETAIL & SCALE, 1/72nd SCALE, COPYRIGHT DRAWING BY LLOYD JONES

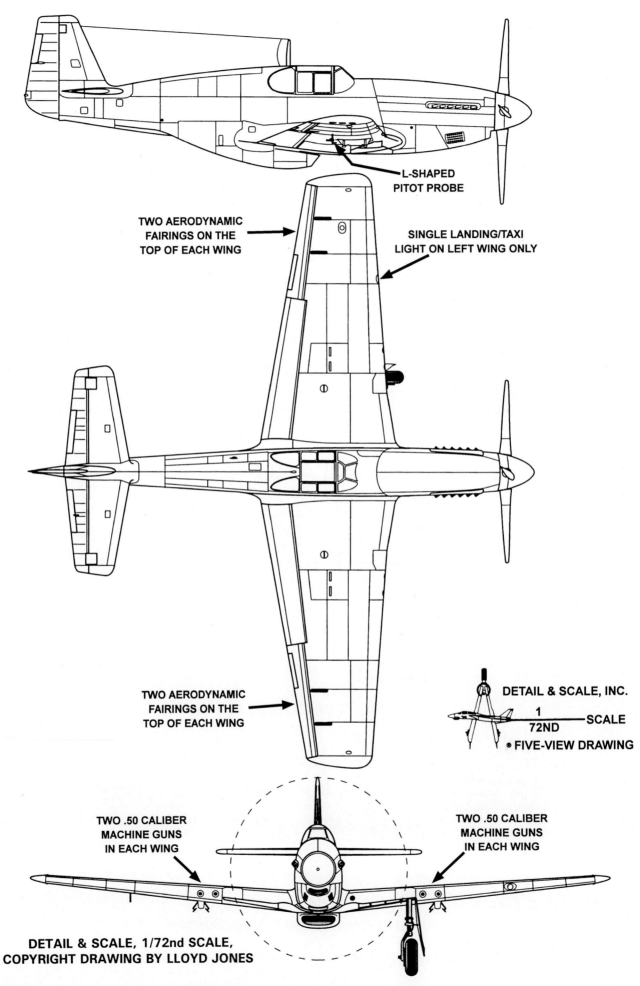

L-SHAPED
PITOT PROBE

TWO AERODYNAMIC
FAIRINGS ON THE
TOP OF EACH WING

SINGLE LANDING/TAXI
LIGHT ON LEFT WING ONLY

TWO AERODYNAMIC
FAIRINGS ON THE
TOP OF EACH WING

DETAIL & SCALE, INC.

$\dfrac{1}{72\text{ND}}$ SCALE

FIVE-VIEW DRAWING

TWO .50 CALIBER
MACHINE GUNS
IN EACH WING

TWO .50 CALIBER
MACHINE GUNS
IN EACH WING

DETAIL & SCALE, 1/72nd SCALE,
COPYRIGHT DRAWING BY LLOYD JONES

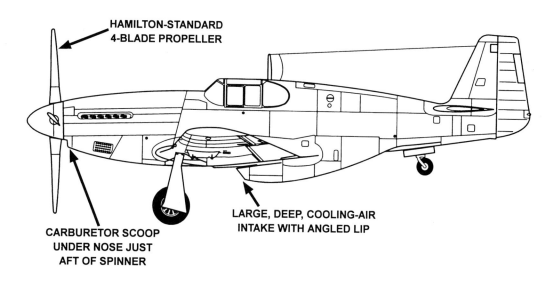

HAMILTON-STANDARD
4-BLADE PROPELLER

CARBURETOR SCOOP
UNDER NOSE JUST
AFT OF SPINNER

LARGE, DEEP, COOLING-AIR
INTAKE WITH ANGLED LIP

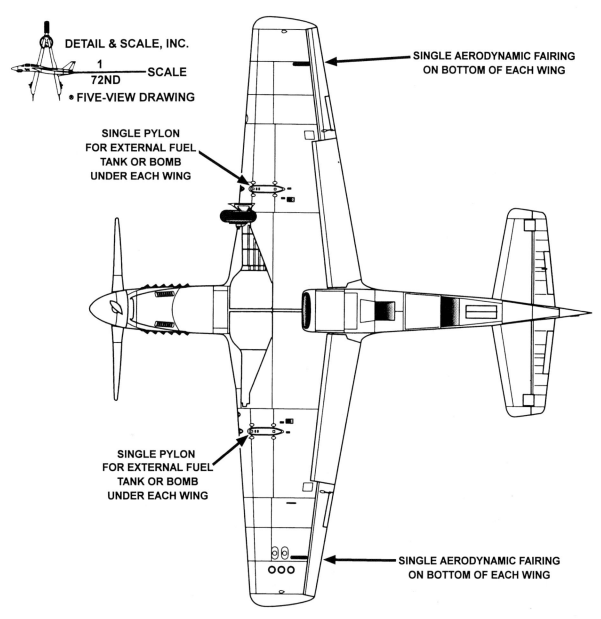

DETAIL & SCALE, INC.

1
——— SCALE
72ND

● FIVE-VIEW DRAWING

SINGLE AERODYNAMIC FAIRING
ON BOTTOM OF EACH WING

SINGLE PYLON
FOR EXTERNAL FUEL
TANK OR BOMB
UNDER EACH WING

SINGLE PYLON
FOR EXTERNAL FUEL
TANK OR BOMB
UNDER EACH WING

SINGLE AERODYNAMIC FAIRING
ON BOTTOM OF EACH WING

DETAIL & SCALE, 1/72nd SCALE, COPYRIGHT DRAWING BY LLOYD JONES

MODELERS SECTION

Note: Only those model kits of the Mustang variants covered in this publication are reviewed in this section. These include the Mustang I through the P-51C. Reviews for kits of P-51D and subsequent variants of the Mustang can be found in The P-51 Mustang in Detail & Scale, Part 2. Because the P-51B and P-51C were identical, P-51B models covered below can also be built as P-51Cs.

1/144th SCALE KIT

Revell (Germany) P-51B

The only 1/144th scale model of a flush-canopy Mustang is from Revell of Germany. It is available through Revell (USA) in the United States.

For the most part, the shape and outline of this kit are very close to what they should be. The one major problem is that the dihedral of the wings is far too great. Simply bending them to the correct angle will result in gaps at the wing roots that are very hard to fill. About the only thing that will really work is to saw the wings in half at the centerline, remove about 1/50th of an inch, then cement the wings in place at the proper angle. Some filling and sanding will still be needed, however.

As might be expected for such a small model, there isn't much detailing. Each main landing gear is one piece, with the strut, outer door, wheels, and tire all molded together. This was done quite well, and is satisfactory for a 1/144th scale Mustang. The inner main gear doors are molded as part of the underside of the wing, so this leaves very little of the main gear wells exposed. No detailing is really needed here. But there is a small piece of plastic which runs chordwise across the opening for each main gear well just inboard of the strut. These pieces of plastic should be removed.

There are drop tanks to go on the pylons under the wing, and these are nice additions to the model. The propeller, spinner, and clear canopy are accurately represented. Scribing is raised and basic, but it is delicate and well executed. Surface detailing even includes the fairings just forward of the ailerons that were added to Mustangs beginning with the P-51B. The exhausts, which are molded into the sides of the fuselage, look accurate and in scale.

There is no detailing in the cockpit, but with the

For the Mustang variants covered in this book, this Revell P-51B is the only kit that is available in 1/144th scale. The dihedral of the wing is excessive, and this needs to be corrected. Otherwise, it is a very good kit for such a small fighter. The author built this one in the markings of the 366th Fighter Squadron from the 4th Fighter Group.

flush canopy painted and glued in place, nothing inside the cockpit is really visible. Missing from the exterior of the aircraft are the radio mast, the L-shaped pitot head, and the landing/taxi light on the left wing. The mast and the pitot head can be made from very thin scrap plastic card. For the light, it is a simple matter to cut a small C-shaped hole in the leading edge of the left wing, then fill it with a drop of clear liquid wax or Kristal Kleer.

For the growing number of modelers who build in 1/144th scale, this is basically a very good kit for a small, World War II fighter. With a little work to correct the dihedral of the wing and the addition of some missing details, it can be built into a very attractive model.

1/72nd SCALE KITS

Airfix P-51B

As one of the older Mustang kits still available, this model is not as detailed as the more recent issues. But its shape and outline are reasonably accurate, and it does not have the correct wing for the P-51B.

Most modelers will want to do some detailing work. Airfix left out the L-shaped pitot head, so one will have to be made from scratch or taken from the spares box. There is also no landing/taxi light provided, but a C-shaped hole cut into the leading edge of the wing and filled with Kristal Kleer will easily solve this problem. When making this hole, be sure to note that the clear cover for the light extends further back on the underside of the wing than it does on the upper surface.

Many modelers will also want to open the carburetor scoop under the spinner. The hot air exhaust ramp is molded in the closed position. This is not incorrect, because this ramp can be left closed on the real aircraft. But it could be changed to the open position with the use of some plastic card.

Care must be taken with the main landing gear which is very fragile. The struts themselves can hardly take the weight of the model until the outer doors are glued in place. Once these doors are added to the struts, they add strength and rigidity, and the landing gear becomes sturdy enough for the model. The main gear wheels are marginally too large, but they could be replaced or sanded down a little to the correct diameter. There is no detailing in the wheel wells, so we recommend building the model with the inner main gear doors in the closed position. This leaves very little of the wells exposed and in need of detailing.

Scribing is raised, but it is very fine. All surface detailing, to include the representation of the control surfaces, is better than average and generally accurate.

There is almost no detailing in the cockpit. Only a floor, seat, and pilot are provided. If the canopy is left in the closed position, all the modeler needs to add is an instrument panel decal, a control column, some seat belts and shoulder harnesses for the seat, and a few pieces of plastic card to represent the larger details on the sides of the cockpit. We spent about fifteen minutes detailing the cockpit of our review model, and it looks quite satisfactory through the closed canopy. The canopy itself is not too thick, and the scribing for the framework is accurate.

Because there is no accurate model of the P-51B/C presently available with today's standards of

Although it has been around for some time, the Airfix 1/72nd scale P-51B is a good kit. It is accurate in outline, but it does lack detailing. The author used Duane Beeson's markings from the 334th Fighter Squadron for this model.

detailing and surface scribing, this model is one option available to the scale modeler as a starting point from which to build these two Mustang variants.

Frog, P-51A

This is a very old kit which is no longer generally available. It is crude by today's standards, and there are several inaccuracies. We include it here only because there is no other injection-molded kit of the P-51A in 1/72nd scale.

It is difficult to tell exactly which version of the Mustang Frog was trying to represent. No armament is represented, and that basically leaves out the P-51 or Mustang IA with their large 20-mm cannon. Likewise, there are no chin guns provided, so the Mustang I and A-36 can be eliminated. Since this clearly is an Allison-engined Mustang, the only remaining possibility is the P-51A. But there is scribing for landing/taxi lights on the leading edges of both wings, and that is not correct for the P-51A. We decided that this was simply an error, and we removed these lights. In building the model, we added the correct single light on the leading edge of the left wing. Holes for the wing guns were also drilled out.

The major problem with the shape of the model is that the fuselage around the cooling-air scoop is too shallow. There is not much that can be done to correct it very easily, but it is not too noticeable unless you have a correct model or scale drawings next to it for comparison.

Shape problems also exist on the wings as well. The tips are too rounded, and should be sanded to the correct outline as illustrated in the drawings in this book. Frog also added the leading edge fillet that was not used on Mustangs until the P-51D. Fortunately, there is enough plastic in the leading edge of the wing to sand this to the correct shape without cutting into the main wheel wells.

The carburetor scoop on top of the nose is too thin, being more like the one used on the Mustang I and P-51. Some plastic card and putty will help here. The cooling-air inlet under the fuselage is way too shallow, so it should also be built up with plastic card and putty. The exhausts are too small. One option here is to remove

them, cut a hole in each side of the fuselage, and use exhausts from the Hasegawa P-51B kit.

Surface scribing is raised, and it is far too heavy. Considerable sanding will be required to get it to an acceptable level. Particularly bad are the ribs on the rudder.

If you have one of these kits and want to build a P-51A, we suggest that you also get a Hasegawa P-51B or P-51C and use parts from it. The landing gear, hot air exit ramp, cockpit detailing, exhausts, wing pylons, drop tanks, and other parts can be used to detail and correct the Frog kit.

To improve the landing gear, remove the tail gear doors and replace them with thin plastic card. There is no detailing in the main gear wells, so build the model with the inner doors in the closed position. This will cover most of the wells and reduce the amount of detailing required by about eighty percent. The main gear itself is decent, but it might also be best to replace it with the more detailed landing gear from a Hasegawa P-51B kit.

The underside of the aft fuselage requires some work too. The hot air ramp is incorrect and must be removed. It is very easy to construct an accurate one using plastic card or use the one from the Hasegawa kit.

Frog provided a nice seat for the cockpit, but there is little else that is usable. Here again, parts from the Hasegawa kit can be used to add details. The instrument panel area will require a lot of attention. Plastic card can be used to make some details that cannot be obtained from the Hasegawa kit. Do not use the Hasegawa floor, because the cockpit floor in the P-51B was covered with plywood. In the Allison-powered Mustangs, the cockpit floor was the top of the metal wing structure.

Simply stated, this is not a very good kit. Many hours of correcting and detailing are required to build an acceptable model. It is unfortunate that no major model manufacturer has recognized the need for producing quality Allison-powered variants of the Mustang. These are important aircraft with interesting histories. With the success of the Accurate Miniatures 1/48th scale kits of these aircraft, hopefully a manufacturer will soon provide these much-needed kits in 1/72nd scale.

The old Frog kit was the first injection-molded model ever issued of the P-51A/Mustang II in 1/72nd scale. It has some shape and outline problems, most of which can be corrected. The author used decals from several sources to build this model of Col. Phil Cochrane's P-51A when he was the commander of the 1st Air Commando Group in the China, Burma, India Theater during 1944.

Hasegawa P-51B and P-51C

The most recently released P-51B/C kits are from Hasegawa. They have beautifully detailed recessed panel lines and good detailing. Fit is excellent, and very little filling and sanding is required during construction.

But Hasegawa made a mistake during its research that resulted in a significant inaccuracy in this kit. The planform of the wing is the one used on the P-51D with the large fillet on each leading edge at the root. Unfortunately, the main gear wells extend into these fillets on the underside, thus making it impossible to simply sand the leading edge of the wing to the correct shape. Regardless of how nice a kit goes together, it is unacceptable to many modelers to have such a noticeable inaccuracy on a finished model. A poll of several dozen modelers taken by Detail & Scale indicated that over ninety percent preferred the more accurate Monogram 1/72nd scale P-51B over this better-fitting and more up-to-date model from Hasegawa.

Recognizing the problem with the wing, Hawkeye Designs produced a replacement set of resin wings along with resin interior details, separate wing flaps, and corrected wheel well doors. The cost of this kit is more than the expensive Hasegawa model, so the modeler must be willing to spend a lot of cash in order to correct Hasegawa's mistake. A more economical alternative is to use Hasegawa's detailing parts to improve the older but more accurate Monogram 1/72nd scale P-51B.

Although not as noticeable as the incorrect wing, the main wheel wells are way too shallow. While some consideration must be given to the scale thickness of plastic as compared to the real thickness of sheet metal, these wheel wells are still much too shallow for the model. What makes this so difficult to understand is that the original Hasegawa 1/72nd scale P-51D had deep wheel wells that looked very realistic. But their subsequent releases of the P-51D and these P-51B/C kits all have the shallow wells. Another small inaccuracy on the underside of the wings are the shell and link ejector holes. There should be one large and two small holes under each wing. Refer to the drawings and detailed photos in this book to make the necessary correction.

For the cockpit interior, there is a nice seat, cockpit floor, and control column, all of which are accurate. However, the detailing on the cockpit sides is poor. Painting these features will be sufficient if the canopy is left closed, but more detailing will be required for an open canopy. Taking the time to add even basic seat belts will also improve the appearance of the cockpit.

Fit is excellent throughout. A little sanding is required on the carburetor scoop underneath the nose and on the cooling-air inlet. There are some ejector pin marks on the main gear wheels, seats, and a few other parts. A little sanding will easily remove these as well. The upper inner surface of the hot air exit ramp is molded into the fuselage, and this results in some slight exterior sink marks on the fuselage halves. A little putty and sanding will remove these. The exit ramp is a separate piece and may be assembled in any position from fully open to fully closed.

Hasegawa provided a choice between the 108-gallon and 75-gallon external fuel tanks. Save the ones you don't use for other kits. They are the best tanks available for the Mustang in 1/72nd scale. Another option is that both the shrouded and unshrouded exhausts are included. Save the one you don't use for possible use on another kit.

The propeller is a work of art, and although it consists of six pieces, it is easy to build. Likewise, the landing gear is delicate, well detailed, yet strong enough for the model.

This kit has been released several times, with some issues having the standard flush canopy and others having the Malcolm hood. It is unfortunate that both are not included in each release. The design of the canopy is interesting. Part of the rear fuselage is included in the clear piece. Once the canopy is glued in place, the modeler simply paints the fuselage section of the piece the appropriate color while leaving the rear windows clear. Also, as is the case with many Hasegawa models, the canopies are not designed to be displayed in the open position to reveal the cockpit interior. Some cutting with a razor saw will be required if the modeler wants to open any of the canopies. Squadron makes thin vacu-formed standard canopies for this kit which are easier to build in the open position.

This is basically a quality kit, but its value is considerably diminished by a major inaccuracy. The wings are on a separate sprue tree by themselves. Hopefully, Hasegawa will rework this tree and correct both the inaccurate wing shape and the shallow wheel wells at the same time. The fact that these problems are very difficult for the modeler to correct makes it important that the manufacturer make the necessary corrections. Considering the high price of this kit, the modeler has a right to expect that Hasegawa correct its mistakes.

Walt Fink contributed to this review.

M News A-36

A new company producing plastic models is M News from the Czech Republic. One of their first kits was a limited production 1/72nd scale A-36. This model is rather crude, and parts are covered with flash. It is poorly engineered, and at first glance, it might not seem worth building. But the shapes are generally correct, and surprisingly, the panel lines are engraved. This allows for considerable sanding which is necessary during construction.

The flash makes many of the small parts unusable, and this is probably just as well, because most of them are crude and inaccurate.

Walt Fink used the Hasegawa 1/72nd scale P-51B kit to build this model of Lt. Eckfeldt's "Bald Eagle." The inaccurate wing is visible in the photograph. *(Fink)*

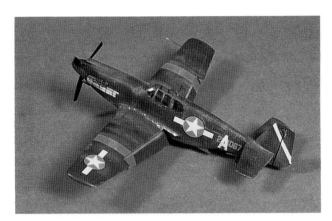

The M News 1/72nd scale A-36 is a rough limited production kit. The author did a lot of extra work and used several parts from Hasegawa and Monogram P-51B kits to build this model of an Apache from the 27th Fighter Bomber Group.

We decided to build this kit using only the fuselage halves, the tops and bottom of the wings, the rudder, horizontal stabilizers, spinner, and propeller. Almost all of the other parts, to include the landing gear, exhausts, cockpit interior, radio antenna mast, pylons, and hot air ramp were taken from a Hasegawa P-51B. Bombs came from a Monogram P-51B, while the chin guns were found in the spares box. The pitot probe was made from a straight pin, and the clear cover for the dual landing/taxi lights was made from a piece of a clear toothbrush.

During basic construction, we cut the main gear wells out of the lower wing of the Hasegawa kit. With some trimming, we got this to fit inside the wings of the M News kit. This added some depth to the shallow Hasegawa wells. While the reworked wells still were not quite deep enough, they certainly were not as shallow as molded in the Hasegawa kit. We also added the Hasegawa hot air ramp to the underside of the fuselage, and we used the Hasegawa tail wheel in place of the one provided in the M News kit. Inside the cockpit, we used several of the parts from the Hasegawa kit as well as making some details from scratch.

The cooling-air scoop does not have the small dip in the center of the upper lip, but this is easy to correct with some scrap plastic. Before gluing the wings together, we cut the flaps from the top wing panels. The groove at the leading edge of each flap was filled and sanded, then they were set aside to be added later.

The fit is only average at best, so considerable filling and sanding is necessary. The holes for the guns are not in the wings, so they must be drilled out. No landing/taxi lights are provided. The best way to add this obvious feature is to cut a notch at the appropriate place in the leading edge of the left wing. Epoxy a piece of plastic cut from a clear toothbrush into this notch. Once the epoxy has set, sand the clear piece to shape, then polish it out.

With a little trimming, the thin, clear, Hasegawa canopy can be made to fit this kit, thus replacing the thicker and rather cloudy one that M News provides.

With the Hasegawa main wheel wells mounted inside the M News wing assembly, it is a simple matter to use the Hasegawa main gear struts, doors, and wheels.

The Monogram bombs fit the Hasegawa pylons with only a little trimming.

Simply stated, this kit will not produce an acceptable model straight from the box. But by following the steps we have outlined here, it can be turned into a very nice model. We were very pleasantly surprised at how well our finished A-36 turned out. At present, this is the easiest way to build an A-36 in 1/72nd scale.

M News Mustang I and Mustang IA

This kit is essentially the same as the A-36, and it requires the same extra work and detailing parts as we described above. The bombs, included in the A-36 kit, have appropriately been deleted, but the pylons remain. The instructions show these pylons being added under the wings, but neither the Mustang I nor the Mustang IA were fitted with them. Two pair of 20-mm cannon have been added for use with the Mustang IA.

To build the Mustang I, the modeler must drill out the holes in the wing guns where the appropriate fairings are located. The chin guns are simply thin plastic dowels, and they should be replaced with better ones from the spares box.

For the Mustang IA, it is necessary to cut out sections from the leading edge of each wing and glue the cannon in place. A separate, bulged, clear piece is provided for the left, rear, cockpit window. But again, the modeler must cut away the window on the canopy, then add this optional piece. A rather phoney looking camera is provided for the rear of the cockpit.

For either version, the modeler must add the landing/taxi lights on the leading edge of each wing. This can be done by cutting C-shaped holes in the correct locations. Fill these with Kristal Klear to represent the covers for the lights.

Since the Mustang IA was the same as the P-51 and F-6A, this kit can also be built with USAAF markings. It will take a lot of work and replacement parts from other kits, but as with our A-36 model, the final results can be well worth it. These limited production M News kits leave a lot to be desired, but they are presently the only ones on the market of Allison-powered Mustangs in 1/72nd scale.

Monogram P-51B

While the Hasegawa kit may offer better fit and recessed panel lines, this thirty-year old Monogram kit remains the most accurate P-51B in 1/72nd scale. This is simply because Monogram got the shape of the wing (and the rest of the model) correct. The panel lines are raised, but are very fine and accurate.

Options include a choice between the standard or Malcolm canopies. But if the Malcolm hood is chosen, the modeler will have to cut the center portion of the standard canopy away, leaving the windscreen and rear windows as separate pieces. This is rather simple if care is taken. Another choice can be made between the 108-gallon drop tanks and 500-pound bombs.

When this kit was released, far less emphasis was placed on interior detailing than it is today. There is no interior to the wheel wells, and only a seat, pilot figure, and control column are included for the cockpit. A decal, which is supposed to be cut out, rather than removed with water, provides the details of the instrument panel.

Monogram did make a couple of errors in their

The older Monogram 1/72nd scale P-51B is not as "state-of-the-art" as the Hasegawa kit when it comes to detailing and fit, however it is more accurate. More than twenty years ago, the author used the Monogram kit to build this model of Don Gentile's "Shangri-La."

research. There are two shell ejector chutes under each wing. There should only be one hole for the shells and two small holes for the links under each wing. As with all 1/72nd scale Airfix and M News kits, the landing/taxi light on the left wing is missing. Again, the simple way to add this is to cut the C-shaped hole at the appropriate location, then fill it with a few drops of Kristal Kleer.

Another error was on the decal sheet. This kit was issued several times with markings for *OLE II*. The correct fuselage codes for this aircraft are YF*I. Its serial number was 43-6928, and it was flown by Lt. William Hodve during March and April 1944. It was assigned to the 358th Fighter Squadron of the 355th Fighter Group. Monogram provided OS*I codes and a serial of 43-112190.

This kit leaves something to be desired as far as detailing is concerned, but the Hasegawa kit has accuracy problems. Perhaps the best model can be made by combining parts from both kits. It would take some effort, but it is the only way to build a 1/72nd scale P-51B or P-51C that is both detailed and accurate.

1/48th SCALE KITS

Accurate Miniatures P-51

Note: Accurate Miniatures has released kits of the P-51, P-51A, A-36, a British Mustang IA, and a P-51B/C. We will completely review the P-51 kit, then explain the differences between that kit and the releases of the P-51A, A-36, Mustang I, and P-51B/C.

In 1994, Accurate Miniatures released three 1/48th scale Allison-powered Mustangs as its first model aircraft kits. These were of the P-51, P-51A, and A-36, and they were followed in 1995 by a British Mustang Mark IA, and in 1996 by a P-51B/C. The first three quickly caught the eyes of scale modelers everywhere for two reasons. First, there had never been any 1/48th scale models of these Allison-powered Mustang variants before, and second, these were excellent kits. If these were Accurate Miniature's first kits, what would be coming in the future?

Accurate Miniatures is a small company compared

to Revell-Monogram, Hasegawa, Testors, or Tamiya. But it is operated by people who are scale modelers, and this shows in the kits. Pieces are designed for ease of assembly, and their accuracy indicates research by someone who knew something about the aircraft before he started.

These kits are well detailed and very accurate. The P-51 is molded in olive drab plastic and features fine recessed panel lines. Rivets are present, but they are in scale and are found only where they are on the real aircraft. Fit is very good, and only a small amount of filling and sanding is required.

The fuselage is molded in four pieces which are attached to one of three sprue trees. These pieces include left and right nose sections that are necessary so Accurate Miniatures could provide different nose pieces as required for the different carburetor scoops and for the A-36's chin guns. But assembly is straight forward, and the sections join at natural breaks in the fuselage panels.

A second sprue tree contains the wings, and several other parts that will vary from variant to variant. In this case, the wings with the mounts for the four 20-mm cannon, the correct four shell ejection slots for these weapons, and the two single landing/taxi lights are included. With them are the four cannon barrels, carburetor scoop, hinged cooling-air inlet, and L-shaped pitot. This sprue tree varies as necessary between the different kits.

The third sprue tree holds the common parts that are included in all of the kits. These include the spinner, propeller, landing gear, horizontal stabilizers, exhausts, and pieces for the cockpit interior.

The cockpit is well detailed, and the floor is correctly represented as the top of the center wing section. Details on the cockpit sides are separate pieces, and additional detailing parts go on the left side. The instrument panel is a clear part, and two options are available. The modeler can simply paint the part black and apply a decal, or he can detail the part using various colors of paint but leaving the "glass" on the instruments clear. If this is done, the decal for the instruments is placed on the back of the panel to show through the "glass." This is one example of how it helps to have modelers designing the kits.

The landing gear is also well detailed. A deep main gear well is molded as one piece integral with the bottom wing piece. Another point that modelers will appreciate is that the wheels and the tires are separate pieces, and this makes painting them much easier. It is a point other model manufacturers should note. As an option, both round and weighted tires are included.

The sprue of clear parts is common to all kits, and it includes two windscreens, standard and Malcolm canopies, rear cockpit windows, and all of the landing lights for the different versions. As mentioned earlier, the instrument panel is also on this clear sprue tree. The reason for the two windscreens is that most P-51As had a small window on the left panel. One of the windscreens has this panel, while the other does not.

Among the few shortcomings is that neither the standard nor the Malcolm canopies can be displayed in the open position as they come in the kit. The standard canopy could be cut with a razor saw and assembled in the open position, but the Malcolm hood is not wide enough to fit over the fuselage and rear windows. By chance, we took a Malcolm canopy from a Monogram P-

51B kit, and it was the correct size to fit on the Accurate Miniatures models in the open position.

Another problem with this kit is that the recoils on the 20-mm cannon are marginally oversized. A little sanding will bring these down to size. It would have also improved the kit if the flaps had been molded as separate pieces so they could be displayed in the lowered position.

By far, the worst feature of the kit is the instruction sheet. It is poorly drawn and difficult to follow, particularly for the landing gear. The exact place where some of the parts join is not clearly indicated. Painting instructions are clear, and Federal Standard numbers are provided for the colors where applicable.

Accurate Miniatures Mustang IA

This kit is virtually the same as the P-51 covered immediately above, but it is molded in light gray plastic. On the tree with the four fuselage pieces are a few extra parts. These include a different deck for the rear of the cockpit and a camera installation. There is also a rear-view mirror to go at the top of the windscreen frame. On the sprue of clear parts is an extra left rear cockpit window with a hole for the camera.

Accurate Miniatures was the first model manufacturer to offer 1/48th scale kits of Allison-engined Mustangs. This is their P-51 model with kit decals. **(Parker)**

Accurate Miniatures P-51A

Different wings come in this kit with the appropriate changes required for the P-51A. These include the single landing/taxi light on the left wing and the four machine guns in place of the 20-mm cannon. The correct shell ejection chutes are on the underside of the wings, but there is only one of the two link chutes under each wing. The barrels of the machine guns are separate pieces that fit in the holes in the leading edge of the wing. This is a better arrangement than having the barrels molded inside the holes or left out entirely.

The P-51A had under-wing pylons, and these are provided as are two 75-gallon external fuel tanks. The scoop for the cooling-air intake is different in that it does not have the panel lines of the hinged inlet. The carburetor scoop is wider than those provided in the P-51 and Mustang IA kits, indicating the presence of an air filter.

For most P-51As, the windscreen with the small window in the left panel should be used. Carefully check your reference material as to which windscreen is appropriate for the specific aircraft you are modeling.

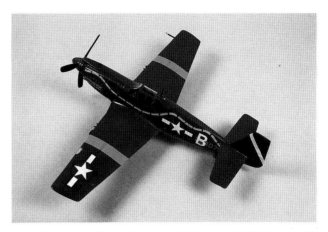

Stan Parker used the Accurate Miniatures A-36 kit to build this model of an Apache from the 27th Fighter Bomber Group. **(Parker)**

Accurate Miniatures A-36

The A-36 requires a lot of new and different pieces, although the basics remain the same. The wings have the dive brakes molded and scribed into them, and it would have been nice if these had been separate pieces. The spaces between the vanes of the speed brakes are open as they should be, but this means you can see into the hollow wing. We suggest gluing a piece of thin plastic card on the inside of the wing opposite the brake to eliminate this problem.

The large, dual, landing/taxi light is correctly represented in the leading edge of the left wing. The lens cover for this fixture is on the clear sprue tree in all the kits, so it is just a matter of choosing the correct one and gluing it in place. Finally, the pitot boom is included to go in the hole in the leading edge of the right wing. The four wing guns are the same as found in the P-51A kit.

The two nose pieces for the fuselage are also different, in that they have the holes for the chin-mounted machine guns. The guns themselves are simply barrels which push back into the holes to a stop. The carburetor scoop is the wider variety as it should be.

Like the P-51A, the A-36 kit has under-wing pylons, but instead of external fuel tanks, two 250-pound bombs are provided. These are exceptionally well executed, and each consists of six pieces.

Dave Pluth contributed to the reviews of the Accurate Miniatures P-51, P-51A, and A-36 kits.

Accurate Miniatures P-51B and P-51C

While the wing, landing gear, and many of the details in this kit remain the same as in the P-51A, Accurate Miniatures had to make a lot more changes to their basic model to come up with their excellent P-51B and P-51C kits.

There are four major parts to the fuselage again, but this time it is the tail section that is separated. Two different tail sections are provided, one with the dorsal fillet, and one without. If the one without the fillet is chosen, the very front part of the fillet must be sanded off the fuselage spine.

Accurate Miniatures provided a well detailed

cockpit with the differences between the Allison and Merlin powered variants correctly represented. Most important of these is the plywood floor that was added over the center wing section on Merlin-powered Mustangs. The fuselage fuel tank is attached to the aft end of the floor, and the radio gear mounts to the top of the tank. The top of the hot air exhaust duct is also part of this piece.

New parts for the cockpit sides also include the necessary differences. The instrument panel changed very little from one Mustang variant to another, so the clear part is again provided for this kit.

Once the basic fuselage parts are assembled, the correct scoops for the carburetor and radiator are glued in place. There is a choice between the shrouded and unshrouded exhausts. The Hamilton-Standard propeller and spinner are accurate and the design of the three parts makes for easy assembly.

Because Accurate Miniatures used the wings from their P-51A kit, the small aerodynamic fairings just ahead of the ailerons are missing. This is unfortunate, because they were added during the P-51B/C production run, and retrofitted to aircraft without them. Therefore, almost all examples of these versions had them. For our review sample, we made these from thin plastic card. It was quick and easy to do, but these fairings should have been included in the kit.

This Accurate Miniatures 1/48th scale P-51B was built by the author to represent Captain Richard Turner's "Short-Fuse Sallee." The aircraft was assigned to the 356th Fighter Squadron of the 354th Fighter Group. This fighter group was assigned to the Ninth Air Force.

Monogram P-51B, (Original Issue)

When this kit was first released in 1967, it was arguably the finest 1/48th scale model on the market. It represented the first big step from kits that were merely plastic shapes to those which were really accurate and detailed models. Monogram did not try to make this kit a toy with working features as it had with some of its previous models. Instead, accuracy and detailing were more important. Exemplifying this change in thinking, the wheel wells were enclosed and detailed, and the cockpit had more than just an instrument panel and a seat.

Although it does not match the more sophisticated kits of today, this original Monogram P-51B can still be completed as an outstanding model right out of the box.

In spite of its quality, construction is very simple. Only six steps are necessary to complete the model. Fit is generally good, and only a small amount of filling and sanding is required to get rid of all seams.

The instrument panel is a decal that is to be cut from the decal sheet rather than be removed with water. It is then glued in place in the front of the cockpit. Details on the sides of the cockpit are molded into the fuselage sides. Monogram did an excellent job here, as this detailing is very complete and accurate. The pilot's seat has the shoulder harnesses and seat belts molded on it, so all the modeler has to do is paint them the correct colors. This was one of the first kits to have such detailing.

A cockpit floor is provided, although it does not really represent the plywood floor in the real thing. It can be corrected with relatively little effort if desired. A nicely sculpted pilot figure is included for modelers who want to add some "life" to their model.

Panel lines are raised, but they are very fine and quite accurate. The landing/taxi light is provided in the form of a clear piece, and all position and navigation lights are molded in the plastic. However, the three identification lights under the right wing tip are missing. Two 75-gallon fuel tanks are included as under-wing stores.

In addition to the missing identification lights, one other error is present in this kit and is the same as found on Monogram's 1/72nd scale P-51B. There are two holes in the bottom of each wing representing the spent shell ejection chutes. There should only be one hole for the shells and two small holes for the ammunition links.

Both standard and Malcolm canopies are included as clear parts and both are thin and very clear. If the Malcolm hood is chosen, the modeler must carefully cut the two rear windows from the standard canopy and glue them in place as separate pieces. The Malcolm hood can be assembled in either the open or closed position, and this is a very nice feature. Although it will take some extra cutting, it is relatively simple to cut the standard

This original, Monogram, 1/48th scale P-51B was built by the author more than twenty-five years ago. It represents Major James Howard's "Ding Hao." Monogram has recently released this kit in their ProModeler line after updating it with engraved panel lines, cockpit detailing, and other improvements.

canopy and display it in the open position as well.

For a kit that is thirty years old, this one is very good. Any modeler who still has one unbuilt may want to keep it in the box as a collector's item. But it is also well worth building for anyone wanting to save the high price of the newer kits.

ProModeler P-51B/-C

This is an improved reissue of the Monogram model covered immediately above. In this case, the kit has one major improvement not seen on Monogram kits that have been re-released in the ProModeler series. This model features engraved panel lines in place of the old raised ones. Previously, the cost of changing raised lines to engraved ones was almost as expensive as new tooling, but Monogram has evidently found a cost-effective way of doing this.

Other improvements can be found inside the cockpit. Gone are the raised details on the fuselage sides, and in their place are separate pieces which are more easily painted and detailed. The seat, radio, and floor are all new, and each piece is more accurate and detailed than before. The first-aid kit is molded into the headrest. There is also a molded instrument panel which replaces the decal in the original issue.

Two features, which were previously molded into the fuselage halves, are now separate pieces. These include the exhausts and the hot air exit ramp. Weighted tires are also provided as they are in all ProModeler kits. Actuators for the inner main landing gear doors are nice additions to the kit as well. In the original issue, there were only empty holes in the wings where the guns belong. Unfortunately, this is one shortcoming that was not improved in the ProModeler release.

Most ProModeler kits have included flight crew figures, and in some cases, ground personnel have been provided as well. This P-51B has a different pilot than the original Monogram kit. It is in three pieces, and is exceptionally well detailed. Another ProModeler standard is the instruction sheet which features photographs of the details on real aircraft. This assists the builder in detailing his model.

In this ProModeler kit, Monogram also added the three identification lights that were missing from the underside of the right wing on the original issue. They also corrected the holes for the shell and link ejector chutes under the wing. This is now the only kit to represent these features accurately. In fact, built straight from the box, this ProModeler kit is the most accurate P-51B/C in any scale. It is also the least expensive compared to the Tamiya and Accurate Miniatures 1/48th scale kits.

With releases now available from Accurate Miniatures, Tamiya, and ProModeler, the scale modeler has a choice of three excellent kits from which to choose when building a 1/48th scale P-51B or P-51C.

Tamiya P-51B

Tamiya's P-51B is truly outstanding. It has more features than any other P-51B/C kit, including separate flaps, optional position canopy, shrouded and unshrouded exhausts, and a choice between 108-gallon fuel tanks and 250-pound bombs to go on the pylons.

The engraved panel line detail is superb and very accurate. Inside the aft fuselage is a radiator that can be seen inside the scoop and hot air exhaust ramp.

There is one major problem with this kit, and that is an inaccuracy in the cockpit. During their research, Tamiya evidently did not realize that Merlin-powered variants had a wooden floor in the cockpit. Instead, they represented the floor as the metal top of the wing's center section. This was the floor in the Allison-powered Mustangs but not for the P-51B and subsequent versions. This would be rather difficult to correct from scratch, but by using a True Details cockpit detailing kit designed specifically for this model, the problem with the floor can be corrected and the cockpit detail improved.

The detailing in the cockpit is decent, but not as good as what is found in the Accurate Miniatures kits. Some of the detailing is molded on the sides of the fuselage halves, while other details on the left side of the cockpit are part of the floor. A one-piece pilot figure is included, but it is not as good as what is found in the ProModeler kit.

Tamiya did get the large hole under each wing for the spent shells correct, but the two smaller holes for the links are missing. The muzzles for the gun barrels are molded into the holes in the wings, but it would have been better if these had been supplied as separate pieces.

Tamiya easily has the best clear parts found in any Mustang kit. Optional parts are provided that allow the canopy to be displayed in the open or closed position. This is something that we would like to see from all model manufacturers, particularly in 1/48th scale and larger kits. Another very nice feature is that the flaps are provided as separate pieces, and it is easy to display them in the lowered position. The inner edge of the flaps are accurate, and this is a difficult feature to get right. More often than not, these flaps were lowered when the aircraft was on the ground. This is another feature that should be on all kits, regardless of scale.

Small features, like the wing pylons and the actuators for the inner landing gear doors, are better detailed than those found in other kits. The only shortcoming here is that the interior of the main gear wells is missing some noticeable features. The inner part of the wells is a separate piece, so care must be taken not to

Lonnie Berry used the Tamiya P-51B kit to build this model of Don Gentile's "Shangri-La." This is an outstanding kit with superior fit throughout. The only real shortcoming is that Tamiya incorrectly represented the cockpit floor. "Shangri-La" had red wheels and a red spinner. However, the red paint had been painted over a previously gloss white spinner, and it often peeled off leaving the spinner white. When this happened, there was a jagged, uneven line between the red and the white. (Munkasy)

wind up with a seam line in the wells during assembly. The propeller spinner can also be a problem. This is one of the few places in the kit where fit is not very good. Dry fit the two pieces together first, and sand as necessary to get a good fit before applying any glue. Once the spinner is assembled, the propeller blades fit perfectly. The technique of using a bushing to secure the propeller so it can spin freely is simple and ingenious.

This is an outstanding kit. With a True Details cockpit set to correct the inaccurate floor, this model can be built into a real showpiece with little effort. Tamiya sets the standard where fit is concerned, so this kit is very easy to build. Very little putty is required. In most cases, only light sanding is needed to remove the seams.

Stan Parker and Lonnie Berry contributed to this review.

1/32nd SCALE KIT

Revell P-51B
Only one 1/32nd scale kit has been released of the Mustang variants covered in this book. It is very poor, having major shape and outline problems, poor detailing, and numerous inaccuracies. Anyone wishing to build an accurate model from this kit should also obtain the Eduard detailing set designed for this model and a Hasegawa P-51D kit in 1/32nd scale. He should also be ready to put in a lot of time and effort to correct and detail this large model. It will take many hours and considerable patience to produce an accurate P-51B or P-51C using this kit.

First released in 1969, this model was one of a series of World War II fighters Revell issued during that time frame. Compared to the others, like the P-40 and Spitfire, it and the P-47 were probably the worst. And like most of the other kits in the series, this model is covered with rivets. These will have to be sanded off, and the entire model will need to be rescribed to get the proper scale effect of the panel lines.

The top of the cowling is removable to display the Merlin engine, but the framework around the engine is not accurate. The engine itself lacks appropriate detailing for a model in this large scale. But it really doesn't matter, since the shape of the entire nose section is incorrect. It is too tapered, particularly on top. What is necessary is to cut off the entire front of the aircraft from the leading edge of the wing roots forward. Replace the nose section

The Revell P-51B kit in 1/32nd scale is very inaccurate in shape and requires a great deal of plastic surgery in order for it to correctly represent the real thing.

with a new one cut from the fuselage of the Hasegawa P-51D kit. Fortunately, the cross sections of the two kits are the same where the Hasegawa nose will join the Revell fuselage. Doing this will also allow the Hasegawa propeller to be used. This is necessary, because the one in the Revell kit has blades that are too narrow in chord.

The lower section of the rear fuselage is also incorrect. Remove everything from the tail wheel forward to a point about an inch aft of where the cooling-air scoop attaches to the model. Replace this with the same area that has been cut from the Hasegawa kit.

The wings are generally correct in shape, but there is no landing/taxi light. A section will have to be cut from the leading edge, and a piece of clear plastic needs to be epoxied in place. Sand this clear piece to shape, then buff it smooth. The navigation lights near the tips of the wings are represented only by raised lines. Better ones must be added from scratch.

There are no gun barrels inside the holes in the wings, so the barrels from the machine guns in the Hasegawa kit can be used. The ambitious modeler can even open one or both of the gun bays using parts from the Hasegawa model.

Surprisingly, Revell did not include under-wing pylons or any stores to go on them. Here again, the Hasegawa kit comes to the rescue with both the pylons and a choice of fuel tanks and bombs to go on them.

There are no holes for the shell and link ejection chutes under the wings. These must be cut into the plastic by the modeler. But don't use the raised lines provided by Revell. Add the correct holes as shown in the drawings in this book.

The Revell landing gear leaves a lot to be desired. It is a simple matter to replace both the main gear and the tail wheel with better parts from the Hasegawa kit.

There is a fair amount of cockpit detailing, but it is generally inaccurate and not very well executed. In particular, the seat is very poor. While all of this can be added from scratch, it is easier to use the Eduard detailing set designed for this model. It replaces almost the entire cockpit interior except for the floor and control column. This detailing set also includes other parts to detail the landing gear, radiator, and hot air exhaust ramp.

The clear parts are very heavy. The standard canopy, found in most issues of this kit, was designed to open and close. Revell made this a working feature rather than allowing the modeler to choose between optional positions. As a result, there are hinges molded into both rear windows and the windscreen. They distort the plastic and look very unrealistic. Unless the modeler is ready to make his own clear parts, these hinges must be sanded off, and the resulting scratches must be buffed out. In a Mustang III issue of the kit, a Malcolm canopy is provided. Unfortunately, the hinges remain on the other pieces, so the same problem exists.

The problems with this kit are considerable, and it will take many long hours of work to turn it into an acceptable model of a Mustang. The entire nose section must be replaced, and a large number of other parts need to be corrected, detailed, replaced, or added. Hopefully, a quality 1/32nd scale model of the P-51B will be issued in the future. Until and unless one is, reworking this kit is the only choice available to the scale modeler short of completely scratchbuilding the model.